# Your First Romance

*Also by Tom Silberkleit and Jerry Biederman*

THE DO-IT-YOURSELF BESTSELLER

# Your First Romance

By

Jennifer Blake • Patricia Matthews • Jude Deveraux • Bertrice Small
Norah Lofts • Johanna Lindsey • Alice Morgan • Patricia Hagan
Marion Chesney • Barbara Michaels • Nora Roberts • Lena Kennedy
V. C. Andrews • Barbara Riefe • Virginia Coffman • Barbara Bonham
Malcolm Macdonald • Roberta Gellis • Cynthia Wright • Jennifer Wilde

CREATED BY
*Jerry Biederman & Tom Silberkleit*

WITH AN INTRODUCTION BY
*Kathryn Falk*

St. Martin's Press     New York

*Design by Laura Hammond*

Library of Congress Cataloging in Publication Data
Main entry under title:
Your first romance.
    1. Love stories—Authorship. I. Silberkleit, Tom.
II. Biederman, Jerry.
PN3377.5.L68Y68   1984        808.3′85        83-21256
ISBN 0-312-89790-1 (pbk.)

First Edition

10 9 8 7 6 5 4 3 2 1

# *Your First Dedication*

To _____
*(fill in sentiment)*

_____

_____

_____

# Contents

CONTENTS

## Romance Twenty-one

# *Acknowledgments*

We wish to thank our twenty participating authors, who have so enthusiastically supported this book with their time and creative efforts. The classic story segments presented in this volume are certain to inspire and encourage its readers/writers through their "first Romance."

Thanks go also to Richard Pine, Jared Kieling, and, of course, Kathryn Falk.

# How to Use This Book

*Romance.*

*It's Not Just for Reading Anymore. . . .*

Welcome to the world of Romance. You have just been commissioned to write twenty all-new romantic adventures. Your coauthors? The most popular Romance writers of our time. Never before have so many top Romance writers come together under one cover for one purpose.

*Here's how it works: Your First Romance* has been divided into twenty sections, each represented by one of our selected authors. We call these sections "Romances." Each Romance contains several opening paragraphs, the beginning of an original "mininovel."

*Now it's your turn: You* continue the story where the author leaves off. That's right. Using your own words and imagination, you complete the story, thus collaborating with some of today's greatest Romance writers. We've included enough space to get you going: The rest is up to you. It's that simple.

Ah, but there's a catch. To make things even more exciting, the authors have provided you with several *closing* paragraphs to each story. Your task is to make both ends meet, guiding your story in a sensible, coherent way from start to finish. Be sure to keep in mind the valuable guidelines provided in Kathryn Falk's introduction. Also, don't forget to review the publishers' tip sheets in the back of the book.

After you have completed all twenty Romances, you'll be ready to move on to Romance Twenty-one—the bonus section! This time, *you're* the author writing the beginning/ending paragraphs. Then, go ahead and pass it along for a close friend or relative to complete. Or do it yourself.

Make room Cartland, Rogers, and Dailey—_____ *(your name here)* has arrived!

Enjoy.

Jerry Biederman
Tom Silberkleit

# *Introduction*

## *by Kathryn Falk\**

Ever since Jane Austen wrote *Pride and Prejudice* and Margaret Mitchell sat in her attic and wrote *Gone with the Wind,* and Janet Dailey composed Harlequin Romances from her traveling trailer (featuring every state in the USA!), readers have dreamed of writing a best-selling Romance.

The paperback market today is dependent on original Romance novels, and the demand for new writers has never been greater. Editors are begging for better writers and more manuscripts.

Each month more than one hundred original paperback Romance novels and Teen Romances are published, and they account for approximately 50 percent of any store's paperback sales. Publishers' figures indicate that this market is earning at least a quarter billion dollars in sales. No one knows if the figure "twenty million readers" is still accurate; I assume it's a low one these days. The readership of *Romantic Times,* in response to a questionnaire, reported that women read twenty to forty Romance novels a month. The average reader appears to be approximately forty years of age. She is married, with more than a high school education, and is working in some capacity.

---

*Kathryn Falk, publisher of *Romantic Times,* is the author of *Love's Leading Ladies* and *How To Write a Romance and Get It Published.* She is also director of The Romantic Book Lovers' Conference and is considered the official spokesperson of the genre. *Romantic Times:* 163 Joralemon Street, Suite 1234, Brooklyn, New York 11201.

Reading Romances is her favorite relaxation. She has definite preferences and buys novels according to her "taste" for Romance—which is different from her mother's!

There are as many kinds of Romances as there are flavors of ice creams. And just as all ices are cold, all Romances today are hot!

The primary difference between yesterday's Romances and today's is the degree of sustained sensuality. Regardless of the type you try to write, whether it be a Historical Romance, a Romantic Suspense, a Regency, a Contemporary, or a Category Romance, genuine raciness is what the readers require. You must look at the "tip sheets" provided to writers by the Category Romance publishers to understand and follow their specific requirements for characters' ages and careers, the minor characters, and the explicit sexuality (see samples provided). A Silhouette Romance might feature a woman of twenty-four, but Dell Ecstasy or Ballantine prefers an older heroine. You should have this information, including the word count for their series, before writing.

*Your First Romance* could be *your* start to writing a best-selling novel. To get you on your way, some of the top names in the genre have provided you with all original beginnings and endings. Thanks to this book, all you need to do is supply the middle section! Here are some ways to keep the going *easy*.

The beginning of a Romance establishes Who? What? When? and Where?—just as in journalism. This can be pretty frightening to a fledgling author when he or she sits down with a blank piece of paper in the typewriter, but here this legwork is already done for you. Just pretend for a moment that you're a reader. What do you think is exciting enough to come next? What do you want to see happen? Then turn to the ending and learn where and how the lovers get together.

Once your imagination takes hold, get out a notebook, and start plotting the scenes of a story.

*1.* Write down the string of events from beginning to end as you would like to see them happen. Try to be unpredictable. Remember, Romances are "fantasy within the realm of reality." Don't be commonplace with the characters but use recognizable, vivid details, such as cosmetics, the everyday things—cars, insurance, dentist appointments, etc.—to create the realism. Readers don't want grim reality, just enough true life to keep it from being impossible, or as unlikely as science fiction. And sure, there are villains and hardships (this keeps the action rolling), but eventually everything works out for a satisfying and happy conclusion that joins the lovers physically and spiritually.

*2.* The heroine must be likeable and admirable without being perfect. She should have good feelings toward her fellow man. She should be someone you wouldn't mind trading places with for a few hours. And the hero must be masterful, yet vulnerable and tender. No matter what his sense of humor, his degree of attractiveness (a recent hero had a black eyepatch, another cried in a scene), he must always be *perfection* in bed. He must be someone the heroine (and the reader) will fall in love with. He can be mistaken for a rogue, but he's loving and faithful to the heroine, and their union at the end is spiritual. Think Cathy and Heathcliff in *Wuthering Heights.* It also helps, of course, if the hero is wealthy, handsome, and successful.

*3.* Dialogue moves the story along. Don't have too much narrative. The reader lives with the characters when they're talking and interacting, not when *you* are explaining what has happened. It's like someone repeating a romantic telephone conversation with Omar Sharif or Burt Reynolds: It's much more exciting to be on the other end of the line than to hear about what was said.

*4.* Speak the dialogue out loud or into a tape recorder. The ear is your check on how the conversation is sounding. Dialogue must provide information on the action and the characters. The sole purpose of minor characters' dialogue is to reveal more about the hero and heroine. Check the endings supplied in this book. Each one indicates the conclusion to which all this action and dialogue are leading.

*5.* Sensuality. The degree of sensuality depends on which company you want to publish your book. But remember this: Romance is sex with love and commitment. Pornography is sex without love and commitment. Promiscuity is not seen in Category Romances and occurs in only half of the Historical Romances. Readers have said that they want "lots of sensuality, but with one man and one woman." However, many erotic Historicals do depend on the heroine being raped by several men, when she is separated from the hero. You must hook your reader in the very beginning with the sexual tension between the hero and heroine. Then you must tear them apart (otherwise there's no story), and reunite them for their happy ending. But the thread that must always be there is the sustained sensuality, even when they're apart.

*6*. Also, think sensuality when you're deciding on details. The smell of the flowers, the scent of her perfume or his after-shave, the touch of the silk, the rustle of the satin, the sound of the water fountain, the sensations of touch and taste. Once you've filled a notebook with the scenes you wish to create and added the details for each scene—from the color of eyes and hair to the brand of toothpaste—then it's time to put all this information on your mind's "filmstrip." This device is used by Janet Dailey, Bertrice Small, and Rosemary Rogers. Their story—and all the sumptuous details—is on a mental movie film that they can unroll at will. Dailey can even back it up to see if someone stands up or sits down. When you're completely familiar with your "filmstrip," then you sit down with the notebook and begin to write. You must have no distractions; writing Romance means you enter another world that is easily destroyed by a ringing phone or doorbell. Mood music can be played in the background to help you continue feeling highly romantic. This is the moment, in front of the typewriter or pad of paper, that you let your erotic imagination unfold to tell the story you've created on "film," and backed up with facts from a sensational detailed notebook.

*7*. I can't tell you how to describe his blue eyes, but try to come up with expressions other than "as blue as the sky"—or any other cliché you've heard too often before. Study the books written by the authors in this book. See how Malcolm Macdonald writes a love scene—notice how he expresses the passion of the heroine (her innermost thoughts at the moment); follow the formula of Pat Matthews, who usually has the heroine struggling to get back the plantation, or her race horse, who sets her story against a definitive slice of history, and usually creates two men for the heroine to choose from. Bertrice Small is extraordinary in writing unusual sexual scenes and plotting an unpredictable series of intrigues for the heroine. Marion Chesney always creates humor and lightness, particularly in her minor characters, each of whom is peculiar and/or frivolous. Virginia Coffman always manages to pour passion and a great deal of motivation into her characters' lives; Patricia Maxwell/Jennifer Blake is one of the most sensual writers and portrays great Romantic characters. Roberta Gellis is near perfection in combining Romance against authentic historical backgrounds. Barbara Riefe (who's really Alan) gives readers a strong story in both plot and characterizations. Whereas Barbara Bonham, who writes of great women and independence, also gives Historical Romance readers some titillation.

The first draft of a Romance is supposed to be rough. Your task as a beginning author, however, is to get as much down as you can and *finish it*. Then put it away for two weeks. When you next take out your manuscript, you'll notice many mistakes, perhaps long, boring passages and a lack of plot-progressing conversations. This happens to everyone. That is the time to revise.

Keep polishing the manuscript, but don't make major changes. Have someone check to see that you use the active voice. (Don't say, "she was kissed." Say, "James kissed her.") Be certain the subject doing the action is always clear to the reader. Check grammar and spelling. Find a good typist so you can send in a clean and neat manuscript. There is no money available in publishing today for revising manuscripts extensively, so make your manuscript as clean of all errors as possible—be a professional.

To submit your Romance to a publisher or an agent, write a query letter which describes who you are in terms of experience in reading Romances. Outline your plot, describe your story, submit the first three chapters or fifty pages, and be sure to include your name, address, telephone number, and a self-addressed stamped envelope. Try to find out the name of the Romance editor of the publishing house, and put it on the address label.

I wish you all the very best of luck. My publication, *Romantic Times*, will be posting news of writers who are using *Your First Romance* to produce a best-selling Romance. I do hope you're one of them.

*Toujours* Romance,

Kathryn Falk

*The difference between the amateur and the professional is that the amateur talks about it, the professional does it!*
—Bertrice Small

# Romance One

# *Jennifer Blake* *(Patricia Maxwell)*
## (b. 1942)

*The fall I was fourteen, I began
receiving anonymous poems. How
could I, given my temperament, resist
such an approach? I met my poet,
Jerry Maxwell, a few weeks later, and
the summer I was fifteen, we were
married.*

With the publication of *Love's Wild Desire,* Jennifer Blake took her place as one of the most popular and successful Romance novelists in America today. Jennifer Blake is actually the best known pen name of Patricia Maxwell, who has over four million books in print, translated into more than six languages.

Born in a 120-year-old cottage in Goldonna, Louisiana, and delivered by her grandmother under the light of a coal oil lantern, Jennifer spent her childhood in an environment that seemed like a setting from the pages of one of her books to come. Married at an early age, she had three children before she was twenty. During this period she did nothing but care for her youngsters, cook, and clean; yet she always found time to read—seven to eight books a week! Before long, however, Jennifer became dissatisfied with much of the material she read, feeling she could do better herself. So she began writing Gothic Thrillers, using the history and atmosphere of her native Louisiana. Soon afterwards, she was writing the more complex Passionate Historicals for which she is best known, and has occasionally detoured to the Contemporary Romance mainly as a challenge and a change of pace.

Jennifer's secret to creating a successful Romance is this: Develop a story so vivid and exciting that the reader will gladly suspend reality in order to participate in it. The ingredients it should contain are (1) a warm, sympathetic, and intelligent heroine; (2) a dynamic and strong hero with underlying tenderness, one every woman can fall in love with for the duration of the book; (3) conflict caused by outside events, not just a clash of personalities; (4) a situation that is suspenseful and engrossing, as well as titillating; (5) a colorful and interesting background.

Jennifer claims the heroines of her books are usually similar to herself in personality and react to situations as she might. At times Jennifer becomes so involved with her characters and plot that she will suddenly awaken in the middle of the night, compelled to continue her work. She averages five to ten pages a day; it takes her approximately six months to complete a Historical Romance and one month for a Contemporary. Jennifer believes the most important thing one can do after writing a novel is to write another. In her eyes, determination is the prerequisite for success.

Jennifer continues to live in her home state of Louisiana with her husband, Jerry, and four children.

*Pen names:*

Jennifer Blake
Maxine Patrick
Patricia Ponder
Elizabeth Trehearne

*Works include:*

*The Secret of Mirror House* (1970, as Patricia Maxwell)
*Love's Wild Desire* (1977)
*Bayou Bride* (1979, as Maxine Patrick)
*Tender Betrayal* (1979)
*The Storm and the Splendor* (1979)
*Captive Kisses* (1980, as Maxine Patrick)
*Golden Fancy* (1980)
*Embrace and Conquer* (1981)

*Royal Seduction* (1983)
*Naked Under the Moon* (1984)
*Midnight Waltz* (1984)

# *Legacy of Desire*

## by Jennifer Blake

and _____
*(your name here)*

The gray rain slashed at the carriage, drumming wet and heavy on the roof. Lightning flared in a silver streak, followed by the explosive rumble of thunder. On the box, the coachman shouted and cursed, urging the horses onward through the stormy night.

The maid, huddled under the carriage robe with only her white lace cap and her eyes showing, gave a moan. "Oh Miss Marina, can't we stop?"

Her mistress did not answer, did not seem to hear. The pale gold of her hair shone in the dimness where she had thrown off her bonnet of silk-lined velvet. The oval of her face was grim in the light of the carriage lantern as she clung to the strap, staring out into the darkness. In her gray eyes with their lavender-blue edging around the irises, there was a hint of pain, though it was firmly denied by the willful tilt of her chin, the compressed line of her delicately chiseled mouth. The words that had been screamed at her that morning rang in her mind. Cutting, vile, they had been meant to hurt. *"Your mother was a demimondaine, a common harlot who spread her legs for half the men of Paris and demanded their heart's blood in return. She was insatiable, greedy, cruel, a woman for whom at least three men died fighting for her favors on the field of honor—if a duelling ground can be so termed in such a cause!"*

*(continue story . . .)*

*(continue story . . .)*

*(continue story . . .)*

_____

_____

_____

_____

_____

_____

_____

_____

_____

The hangings stirred at the window, wafting in the draft of cold wind. The flames in the fireplace leaped higher, bathing Marina in their red-orange glow, striking through the lace-edged lawn of her nightgown, outlining the tender curves of her body in a rose-red nimbus, catching gold fire in the rippling cascade of her hair. A prickling ran along her nerves and down her spine. With her breath caught in her throat and the silver-backed hairbrush she held clenched in her hand like a weapon, she turned in a slow pirouette.

He stood near the window embrasure, his dark clothing blending with the hangings, a look of hunger and despair in his black eyes, though his features were congealed in a bronze mask.

"Justin," she whispered.

"I have come." The words were hoarse, as if dragged unwillingly from his throat.

"I have been waiting, alone."

Then she was locked against his hard body, his mouth upon hers. The fire sank lower, sputtering, murmuring. It crackled and a live coal skittered across the hearth to the rug. It lay there, red and smoking, dying finally, unheeded.

# Romance
# Two

# *Patricia Matthews*

## (b. 1927)

*. . . there is a hunger in people to return to a simpler time, when good and evil were more clearly defined . . .*

Patricia Matthews had been writing Gothic mysteries, fantasy short stories, and juvenile books until her agent one day suggested she try her hand at Historical Romances. So she did, and when her first romantic novel, *Love's Avenging Heart,* rocketed onto the best-seller lists, Patricia knew she was on to something! The book ignited her enormously successful Love Series, which sold over fifteen million copies. Her name has since been a regular on best-seller lists nationwide.

Patricia believes the growing complexity of our society brings with it a greater need for escape and romance, which seem to be lacking in most people's lives. Her stories contain the same ingredients crucial to all good stories: a strong plot and subplot, lots of conflict, and well-rounded characters whom the reader can identify with and care about. Patricia, disliking routine, never writes at precisely the same time each day. Rather, she sets aside a specific quota of pages that must be done by day's end; this, she concedes, keeps her well disciplined. During the course of her day, Patricia can work easily through all distractions and interruptions, and after six months or less of steady writing, the finished product will emerge. Her two important hints to anyone interested in writing Romance are: *1)* Learn to write as well as you can, and *2)* join Romance Writers of America; they give lots of support and information to beginning writers.

A native Californian, whose other interests include novels of suspense, witchcraft, and the occult, Patricia currently lives with her husband on their avocado farm in Bonsall, California. Her husband, and part-time collaborator, is the popular American writer Clayton Matthews. Together, Patricia and Clayton have come to be known as the hottest couple in paperbacks today.

*Pen names:*

P. A. Brisco
Patty Brisco
Laura Wylie

*Works include:*

Love Series (1977–81)
*Love's Avenging Heart*
*Love's Wildest Promise*
*Love, Forever More*
*Love's Daring Dream*
*Love's Pagan Heart*
*Love's Magic Moment*
*Love's Golden Destiny*
*Love's Raging Tide*
*Love's Sweet Agony*
*Love's Bold Journey*
*Tides of Love* (1981)
*Empire* (1982, with Clayton Matthews)
*Flames of Glory* (1983)
*Dancer of Dreams* (1984)

# Love's Seeking Heart

## by Patricia Matthews

and _____

*(your name here)*

The wind was cold. It swirled down the narrow street of the village of Briarly, bringing with it the frail flakes of the winter's first snow, laying them not ungently upon Samantha's hot cheeks, where they quickly melted, leaving a spot of dampness like a lover's kiss.

But neither the wind nor the snowflakes cooled the heat that Samantha felt roiling within her body and mind. How could her father suggest such a thing, and worse yet, how could her mother agree? Things were hard, yes. Food was scarce, and the winter was coming upon them with all that entailed, but to ask her to go to Joshua Squires, to expect her to be his woman, his wife! To give her to a man whose breath was sour and whose face and body sagged with the weight of a bitter old age!

She shuddered, thinking of his touch, and worse. She was only sixteen. Sixteen, and all of her life should be ahead of her. If they made her do this, she would have no life at all. But she would not. They could not force her. She would leave the village first. Death in a snowdrift would be preferable to the embrace of Joshua Squires!

_____

*(continue story . . .)*

_____

_____

_____

_____

_____

_____

*(continue story . . .)*

*(continue story . . .)*

_____

_____

_____

_____

_____

_____

_____

_____

_____

_____

_____

She saw him coming toward her, over the little bridge that spanned the pond, and a thickness that was only partly tears grew in her throat. He had come back. Despite her willful words, despite the hurt she knew she had given him, he had come back. David, with his strong shoulders and gentle hands, with his deep voice and his strength. How could she ever have doubted that it was he whom she loved; how could she have ever thought that another could take his place; how could she have been beguiled by false promises, false declarations of love? All would be well now. They would be together, here in Croyden. She would now have the heart of it as well. A home must have a heart, Samantha had once thought; and now her home would have its heart in the man she loved. Opening the door, she ran toward him, calling his name.

# Romance
# Three

# ABOUT THE AUTHOR

# *Jude Deveraux (Jude Gilliam White)*

## (b. 1947)

*When I wrote my first book, I'd never written
anything before, had no idea there were rules
of writing. I just packed it, sent it to a
publisher and it was accepted.*

Jude Deveraux is actually the pen name of Jude Gilliam White, whose titles
currently total over two million copies in print. Her first novel, *The Enchanted
Land,* set deep in the rich bluegrass splendor of nineteenth-century Kentucky,
was sent to a publisher on the urging of her husband. He persuaded Jude, at
the time an elementary school teacher, to mail forty pages of her manuscript to
New York. Four weeks later word arrived that a contract was being offered.
This marked the beginning of an impressive career as one of America's most
well-known Romance writers.

Born on a farm in Fairdale, Kentucky, Jude spent the first seven years of
her life surrounded by an extended family of grandparents, aunts, uncles,
parents, and chattering siblings. It was not until her family finally left the farm
that Jude discovered the true luxury of solitude. Her flair for writing flourished
during the tranquil hours of the day, as her imagination drifted with the
exploits of pioneers, Indians, and others who had once populated her home
region. Jude declares she began writing Romance novels because Kathleen
Woodiwiss' books didn't come out often enough, and she couldn't find any
other books she wanted to read. So she wrote her own.

Jude is the type of writer who never really knows what the outcome of her stories will be as she is writing them. She claims her characters seem to pop out of her head and call for her to bring them to life on paper. Her heroines have strong minds of their own, refusing to give up their identity to anyone, and they are always women with purpose. Jude likes to think of herself as the old-fashioned type. Her heroines love one man and remain faithful to that man. She believes that luscious sex scenes should be secondary to memorable characters and a good, strong, original story.

Jude's detailed descriptions and historical accuracy have become trademarks of her work. Her research has led her to libraries all over the world. While researching her novels, Jude designs and sews the clothing for several of her main characters, using doll-sized mannequins for models. As part of her commitment to accuracy, she often creates cardboard sets of the buildings and landscapes in her stories. She fills her writing studio with everything she can find to remind her of the particular time period she is writing about. By the time she starts writing, there is hardly an inch of bare floor, desk, or wall space.

Jude's writing studio is the house next door to her home. It generally takes her six months to complete a novel. She will research for four months, then write for two. She prefers to write longhand in pencil (she doesn't even own a typewriter), averaging thirty-five hundred to forty-five hundred words per day, and she is always thinking out new plots—even while in the shower. If she is not persuaded to stop working, she will continue writing for sixteen hours at a time. The long hours spent sitting behind a desk have recently encouraged Jude to start working out with barbells. Jude and her husband, Claude, live in Santa Fe, New Mexico where she nurtures her dream of someday having a writing studio built right into a hillside.

*Pen names:*

Jude Deveraux

*Works include:*

*The Enchanted Land* (1978)
*The Black Lyon* (1980)

*The Velvet Promise* (1980)
*Highland Velvet* (1981)
*Casa Grande* (1982)
*Velvet Song* (1982)
*Sweetbriar* (1983)
*Velvet Angel* (1983)

# *Alicia**

## by Jude Deveraux

and _____
*(your name here)*

Alicia's lovely face was distorted with rage, for in her hand she clutched a crumbled legal document. Sloan Jefferson was suing her for sex discrimination!

She'd met the arrogant Mr. Jefferson six months ago at a cocktail party and immediately he'd started pursuing her with all the subtlety of an express train. Alicia had no desire to be one of the notorious Sloan Jefferson's "harem" of women so she'd said no to every invitation, refused his gifts of flowers, candy, and whatever had been in that black velvet box he'd had delivered. After three months he seemed to have given up—until he showed up in her office.

Alicia'd been interviewing for a new assistant, someone who was free to travel all over the world with her in her job as a textile buyer for a New York design firm. She had to admit that she'd been quite rude when Sloan had applied for the job.

---

*Jude Deveraux's novels are titled by her editor after they are written. Therefore, she suggests you may wish to complete this story first—then retitle it.

*(continue story . . .)*

*(continue story . . .)*

"You're the worst secretary I ever saw," she murmured against his lips.

"But you'll have to admit that I'm not bad as a companion. Our nightly . . . oh . . . entertainments were worth my salary."

"Worth your salary!" she gasped. "What about when you insulted that Turkish rug merchant and nearly got us shot?"

"I didn't like what he was thinking about you," Sloan said stubbornly.

"And how could you know what he was thinking?" she half accused. "No one can read anyone else's thoughts."

"Alicia, my love, look into my eyes and tell me what I'm thinking."

Alicia, to her consternation, blushed.

"Now," he murmured, pulling her to him, "let me *show* you what I'm thinking."

# Romance Four

# *Bertrice Small*

## (b. 1937)

*It's a real blessing to be able to earn a living doing what you love to do, but publishing is a business, and the writer who doesn't realize it is in for trouble. . . .*

A familiar name on best-seller lists, Bertrice Small ranks among the great Historical Romance writers of today. Her novel *Skye O'Malley* was the third Romance ever to be published in the innovative trade size; its massive appeal prompted other publishers to follow the larger-format trend with their top authors.

Bertrice may not have been born with a pen in her hand, but it was soon to become a recognized trademark. At the age of six, she was already writing poetry and short stories. By thirteen, she had written her first Romance. In college Bertrice studied both English and history, but was unable to decide which subject she liked the best. Soon, however, her writing was to provide the perfect solution—combine the two! Bertrice loves to teach history through her books. She believes that the Historical Romance is a way for people to learn history and at the same time enjoy it. Bertrice admits she'd rather spend her time in the past, believing that Romance is marvelous escapism.

All good Romance novels, Bertrice points out, must contain certain basic ingredients including good research, realistic dialogue, and well-drawn characters. A *great* Romance, she says, is one that can heavily involve its readers to the point where they will laugh and cry and want to hiss at the villain. Bertrice prefers not to submit an outline to her publisher. She feels this would bind her characters to follow a preset destiny. Rather, characters should be allowed to take their own lives in hand. As an example, she explains that Francis Stewart-Hepburn, the sixth Lord Bothwell, started out as a minor character in *Love Wild and Fair*. But by the story's end, he had become one of the two heroes. Bertrice has a habit of getting involved with some of the characters she invents. For her these people exist, and as far as she's concerned, it's quite possible that once they really did.

Her first novel, *The Kadin*, was the result of several years of research, writing, and rewriting. Today, she turns out a book a year. Bertrice works best under orderly and calm conditions, and says she prefers a green and white environment highlighted with classic or contemporary mood music. She begins her day at about 11 A.M. and works until the evening, writing only in longhand because the noise of the typewriter is too distracting. Bertrice lives with her husband, George, who reproduces seventeenth- and eighteenth-century clocks for sale in their gift shop, and her son, Thomas David, at their home in historical Southold, Long Island.

*Works include:*

*The Kadin* (1978)
*Love Wild and Fair* (1978)
*Adora* (1980)
*Skye O'Malley* (1980)
*Unconquered* (1982)
*Beloved* (1983)
*All the Sweet Tomorrows* (1984)
*Sweet Surrender* (1985)

# *Passion's Fire*

## by Bertrice Small

### and _____
*(your name here)*

The hoofbeats of a single horse echoed in the damp chill of the mid-September night as they galloped their way up the long tree-lined drive to Graystones Priory. The great house looming ahead in the blackness was dark, its inhabitants long abed. The caped horseman, with a knowledge born of total familiarity, directed his mount around the side of the house and into the stableyard. Dismounting, he walked the sweating, steaming animal until it had cooled down, and only then did he lead the beast to water. His mount properly cared for, the rider tied him to a hitching post and made his way to the house, entering it with his own key through a small, barely noticeable vine-covered door at the side of the building.

Inside he paused a moment, listening closely, almost scenting the air for danger; and then seeing a faint light beneath the library door at the rear of the house he made his way towards it, opening the door without knocking, and stepping into the room. She was standing with her back to the door before the low, orange fire. He closed the door softly with a tiny click, and she whirled, her magnificent violet eyes wide with relief. "Matthew," she whispered, and Matthew, Lord Tarleton, gazed for a moment upon the only woman he had ever loved. His silver grey eyes drank in her perfection, the mass of smoke black hair, the camellia white skin, her tempting breasts visible beneath the thin lawn shift, her adorable pink mouth. He swept her into his arms and fiercely kissed that mouth, his own lips both tender and demanding. Momentarily sated, he lifted his head from hers murmuring, "Velvet, my love, why have you sent for me? You know the danger involved. Until King Charles is restored I am a marked and hunted man."

Velvet Somerton's eyes filled with tears. "I am to be married, Matthew," she said softly. "Father says the Stuarts will never be restored, and we must survive as best we can. I am to be married in two days time to Robert Hadley."

"But you are my betrothed wife," protested Lord Tarleton.

*(continue story . . .)*

*(continue story . . .)*

_____

_____

_____

_____

_____

_____

_____

_____

_____

_____

_____

_____

_____

_____

_____

_____

_____

_____

Charles Stuart had been back in England three months as king when he was approached late one evening in his chambers by a radiantly lovely girl. His first thought was how she had successfully gotten past his guards. The girl curtsied low so he might have a fine view of her lush breasts. She didn't look like an assassin. "I am Velvet Somerton, sire, and I would beg a favor of you." Lazily he let his eyes sweep over the petite creature who stood before him, admiring her marvelous violet eyes and rosebud of a mouth that seemed to be begging for his kisses. He had rarely been known to refuse a lovely woman anything.

"The favor is for Lord Tarleton, sire. He is the man who saved you from an assassin seeking to prevent your return. He is destitute, sire, his lands not being yet restored. He will not ask for himself and would be furious to know that I had asked for him. He believes that what he did was his duty, no more. He is a proud man, sire, but pride will not fill his empty belly." She caught at his hand. "I know that you are besieged with supplicants for many rallied to your majesty's cause, but I would do *anything* to express my gratitude. My father will not allow our marriage until Matthew's lands are restored, and we have waited so long!" Her look was both melting and beseeching.

The king reached out and pulled the tempting girl into his arms. Bending, he kissed the cherry lips she quickly held up to him, and then he eyed her with amusement. "You'd do it, sweetheart, wouldn't you?" he said admiringly. "You'd let me seduce you in order to help your betrothed!"

A feathery eyebrow was delicately raised. *"You seduce me?* I thought 'twas I who was seducing your majesty!"

Astounded, the king's mouth dropped open, and then he began to chuckle. "Madame," he said, "I must refuse your very generous offer for I should ill repay Matthew Tarleton by such an action." Loosing her, he moved to a table, and poured some wine, handing her a goblet. "Velvet Somerton," he said, "you will have your happy ending, I promise you. Now, madame, let us drink to England!"

# Romance
# Five

## *Norah Lofts*

### (1904–1983)

*. . . there are people who can walk*
*a tight rope, or drive motor cars.*
*Telling stories is just something*
*that I happen to be able to do.*

Throughout her life, English novelist Norah Lofts' passion for old houses provided the inspiration for many of her Historical and Romantic novels. She was not typically categorized as a Romance author. To Norah, romance was not exclusively a man-woman relationship. Places and, for her, houses especially, could be romantic. She particularly enjoyed stories that examine triumph over the human predicament. For Norah, boy meets girl was no longer enough. She considered *Gone with the Wind* the prime example of a great Romance. Though its main theme was unrequited love, Norah felt it dealt with much more: a place, a time, a crisis in history.

Characters and situations found in Norah's work had no conscious origin, they just came to her. A blank sheet of paper, a typewriter, and solitude were all she ever required. Norah always warned would-be authors never to embark upon writing without a private income or a steady job. Her message—hope to strike gold, but be grateful for silver.

*Lane End House*, Norah's contribution to *Your First Romance*, was one of her final works before her death. It serves as testimony to her lifelong love affair with old houses, her first romance.

*Pen names:*

Juliet Astley
Peter Curtis

*Works include:*

*Bless This House* (1954)
*Scent of Cloves* (1957)
*The House at Old Vine* (1961)
*Out of the Dark* (1972)
*The Lonely Furrow* (1977)
*Gad's Hall* (1978)
*Haunted House* (1978)
*Day of the Butterfly* (1979)
*Anne Boleyn* (1979)
*The Lost Queen* (1981)
*Requiem for Idols* (1982)

# *Lane End House*

## by Norah Lofts

and _____
*(your name here)*

I should never have seen the house had I stuck to the main road, but one of those know-alls for whom I have an irresistible attraction had suggested a shortcut. Then he had misdirected me, or I had misunderstood him and soon it was apparent that the shortcut was leading nowhere. I began to look for a place in which to turn. And I found it: a farm entry. Turning into it, prepared to reverse, I saw the house, standing back behind a wall and partially sheltered by a vast copper beech. Old, empty, with that peculiar look of desolation that deserted houses have.

I am not a romantic person. I do not see in every man I meet a potential lover. I do not believe in the happily-ever-after that wedding bells promise. But I admit to being romantic about old houses. I think of all the people, the hopes, fears, loves and hatreds, good times, bad times, the living and the dying. . . . Now I felt that I must have a closer look.

It was very old: Tudor or early Jacobean. Cupping my hands about my eyes I peered in through dust and cobwebs and saw beamed ceilings, panelled walls, wide open hearths. I was so engrossed that I heard nothing until a voice, a man's, asked, "Can I help you?" It was not a friendly inquiry; it was challenging.

"N-no. I was just looking."

"Then perhaps *you* could help *me*. I take it it's your car blocking my entry."

"Oh yes. I'm sorry. I'll . . ." I ran back to the car and proceeded to give a shocking display of inept driving. Most unfair, for I am a good driver. I've held a licence for eight years, ever since I obtained one when I was eighteen. Now I stalled the engine, made the car buck, reversed almost into the nose of his tractor. Leaning down from the driving seat he said, "Try going forward." I obeyed and found myself in a wide farmyard. The tractor followed and he jumped down. He was tall, lean, bronzed and had reddish hair, a colour to which I am susceptible, I think because at my very first school the only little boy who wasn't beastly had been a red-head.

"Now," he said, markedly less hostile, "if you'd like to take a proper look, I'll show you over."

I said, "Oh, I would." I've often thought since that had I only foreseen the trouble, the misery, the downright physical danger I was inviting, I might have refused that invitation. But what I should have missed!

---

*(continue story . . .)*

---

---

---

*(continue story . . .)*

*(continue story . . .)*

Alan said, "A good old custom," and lifted me over the threshold and set me gently down. He said, "Welcome home, darling," and turning, said to the little crowd who had followed from the church, "Come in and be welcome." My arm was still in plaster but my multiple bruises were fading. I was able to enjoy my wedding feast.

Somebody—probably a poet—said, "Never the time and the place and the loved one, all together." So how fortunate I must consider myself, with the man I loved, in the house I loved. And time? Well, Alan had said that he might perhaps manage a three-day honeymoon.

# Romance
# Six

# ABOUT THE AUTHOR

## *Johanna Lindsey*

### (b. 1952)

*Romance is the heart of life.*
*Reading about it is the second*
*best thing to living it.*

Johanna Lindsey was only twenty-five years old when her first attempt at writing was published. More remarkably, the book, *Captive Bride,* the result of an attempt by Johanna to write only a scene from a novel for self-amusement, became a major best-seller. Since that auspicious beginning, the young writer, wife and mother of three children, has gone on to produce an impressive string of best-sellers, securing a position as one of America's leading Romance authors.

Johanna's stories originate from a basic idea; the novel is not tied to an outline, but rather is allowed to develop by itself as it is being written. She proposes that writers of Romance attain an intimate relationship with their characters, live with them, suffer and delight with them, and give them the freedom to do as they wish. Further, she feels that if the characters are believable and compelling, anything that happens to them will be of interest. Excitement, adventure, heartache, joy, all of it then falls into place. According to Johanna, a great Romance is easy to recognize: It is a book that has its readers glued to every page, makes them furious if they have to put it down, keeps them tense, makes them laugh or cry. It is a book that they will read again and again.

Johanna, born in Germany, daughter of a master sergeant in the U.S. Army, has spent most of her life in Hawaii, on the island of Oahu. She met her husband, Ralph, on a blind date just after graduating from high school, and married him four months later. Writing occupies all of her spare time when she is not taking care of her home and family. First she does the necessary research at a local library, and then spends the next two and a half to five months writing the book. She does her best work at night, when there is total quiet. Johanna plans to continue writing nonstop, entertaining herself and, of course, her many readers.

*Works include:*

*Captive Bride* (1977)
*A Pirate's Love* (1978)
*Fires of Winter* (1980)
*Paradise Wild* (1981)
*Glorious Angel* (1982)
*So Speaks the Heart* (1983)
*Heart of Thunder* (1984)
*A Gentle Feuding* (1984)

# *Love's Persuading*

## by Johanna Lindsey

and _____
*(your name here)*

"Has he arrived? Can you see him?"

Yvonne Lawrence jumped back from her bedroom balcony, thoroughly embarrassed to have been found out by her young sister, Mary, after she had professed no interest in the mysterious stranger who would soon be their guest. Now Mary was leaning over the balcony, looking eagerly up and down the cobbled street, quiet without the usual passing of smart carriages.

"I don't see him at all." Mary said with great disappointment after a moment. Yvonne lifted her long skirts and flounced back into her bedroom, calling over her shoulder. "I don't wonder, since Mr. Adam Garner isn't due for another half hour. And I wasn't looking for him!" she added sharply.

Mary ran in after her sister, grinning knowingly. "You were too. You can't pretend to me you're not curious. After all, father has made such a big to-do about it all, yet he won't tell us anything about our soon-to-be guest. And he's been so nervous! Since when is father ever nervous about anything?

A good point, only Yvonne wouldn't concede it, not to her bigmouth sister. "Your imagination is working overmuch, Mary. Father is just—well, he's—"

"Go ahead, I dare you to call it anything but nervous."

Yvonne glared at her sister, emerald eyes sparkling. "Get out of here, little imp, so I can finish getting ready!"

"Yes, you do have so much more to do," Mary teased in a most serious tone, gaining another stabbing look from her sister. Yvonne couldn't have looked more beautiful, but Mary would never admit it. "And don't forget father has warned us to be at our best, although good impressions have never worried him before." But Mary frowned then, as she walked slowly to the door, caught up in the mystery again. "You know, father really seems more afraid than nervous."

*(continue story . . .)*

*(continue story . . .)*

*(continue story . . .)*

_____

_____

_____

_____

_____

_____

_____

_____

_____

_____

_____

_____

Yvonne smiled at her reflection in the mirror as she prepared for bed. Such a glowing look she had about her, the result of—she blushed. Would she ever get used to having such a passionate husband? Just thinking about him could excite her and bring color to her cheeks. Yet if someone had told her a year ago that she would end up marrying Adam Garner, she would have called them a liar, and a few other choice names, for even suggesting such a thing. How she had hated Adam then, and his exasperating arrogance. But now she loved him to distraction—she couldn't help it. The mystery was over, and although it had been painful in the solving, she had a new life now, and a love for which she would be eternally grateful.

# Romance
# Seven

# ABOUT THE AUTHOR

## *Alice Morgan*

### (b. 1933)

*It wasn't enough for me to read the hero kissed and caressed the heroine. . . . I wanted to know how he kissed her, where he caressed her, and what he did when they made love.*

Candlelight Ecstasy's Alice Morgan, winner of the 1982 Pearl Award, is one of the most delightful and provocative personalities in the field of Contemporary Romance. Boredom with reading Romance books that took the hero and heroine to the bedroom door only to shut it in the reader's face was Alice's original incentive for buying a typewriter and 200 sheets of blank paper. She was determined to plot stories that would share the characters' intimacies with the reader without restriction. She soon discovered that sensuous love scenes were the most enjoyable part of writing, and with the success of her first book, *Masquerade of Love*, Alice knew the public was ready!

Alice believes the ingredient every Romance should contain is a strong, compassionate, tender hero who is undeterred in the pursuit of his heroine from the very first contact—or vice versa. She feels the heroine must be independent, saucy, and intelligent enough to keep the hero on his toes. Physically stimulating scenes demonstrate an important part of her characters' total personality. Alice feels that sexually explicit words alone do not make an exciting love scene. More important are a couple's constant interaction throughout the story, creating a mood for lovemaking when the occasion arises. Alice's characters and plots originate from a single thought that expands freely and uninhibitedly. She affirms that all of her stories are intermixed with fantasy and real events from her life.

Alice has written in motel rooms, while traveling, touring, during conferences, and in the middle of family gatherings. According to Alice, authors have to be prepared at all times to jot down that special inspiration or thought wherever they are. Depending on the length of the book she is writing, it takes her anywhere from one week to five months to complete her work. Alice prefers to write at night in her oceanfront home and credits her loving husband for providing her with the stimulus to write emotionally stirring Romances.

*Works include:*

*Masquerade of Love* (1982)
*Sands of Malibu* (1982)
*The Impetuous Surrogate* (1982)
*Branded Heart* (1983)
*Man in Control* (1984)
*Deception for Desire* (1984)

## *Conspired Seduction*

by Alice Morgan

and _____
*(your name here)*

One touch of a match brought the waiting eucalyptus logs flaring to life. At the same time there was a brisk knock at the entrance. Keen, serious eyes surveyed the room. Everything was perfect in the studio beach house. The wine was chilled, the refrigerator stocked for a long weekend and the black satin sheets spread smooth over the wide bed. Opening the door, Mike smiled into the wary eyes of the invited guest.

"Come in, please." Boldly locking them in, the key was pocketed.

"What's up, Mike? Why the urgent request to meet you here at this late hour? I see you're already dressed for bed."

Moving forward, Mike paused in front of the burning logs to warn with unmistakable conviction, "I'm going to seduce you."

"You're what?"

"Since I was fourteen I've loved you and for ten long years have waited until the timing was right. I've read every how-to book on the subject and imagined over and over each ardent act I intend to perform. My hands are eager to stroke your wavy black hair, my tongue yearning to invade your mouth until you're gasping for breath, my fingers aching to explore every inch of your enticing body followed by my lips caressing the same erotic path. When I'm through, I assure you, you'll never think of another lover the rest of your life."

"You, er, you don't know what you're saying."

"The hell I don't!" Mike exclaimed in a deep, throaty voice. Both hands raised to untie the tightly looped belt. One shrug of golden-tanned shoulders and the robe lay in a heap on the soft fur rug spread before the fireplace.

Mike stood in the saffron-yellow glow of the fire wearing nothing but clinging ebony-colored Jockey briefs.

"Damn it, Mike, quit this nonsense." Stormy gray eyes stared into luminescent sea-green eyes before lazily trailing from the lustrous auburn hair and determined features, down the satin smooth curves of the near naked form and slowly back up again.

"That's another thing!" Mike chided angrily. "You always call me by the masculine nickname my brother gave me. After I'm through with you tonight, there will be no doubt in your mind that my name is Michelle."

"With your voluptuous body displayed so sensuously, there is no doubt you're one hundred percent female right now," Mark pointed out, walking closer as Mike did with outstretched arms and a rapidly beating heart.

---

*(continue story . . .)*

_____

_____

_____

*(continue story . . .)*

*(continue story . . .)*

_____

_____

_____

_____

_____

_____

_____

_____

Mark touched a match to the waiting logs before standing up to enfold Michelle in his strong arms. He nuzzled her neck, whispering, "Your conspired seduction cost me plenty, you shameless female."

Raising her face, Michelle placed her lips over his in a long, lingering kiss that ignited the constant hunger they felt for each other.

"Other than the cost of our beachfront hideaway, an end to your womanizing life-style and a home in the country, I can't think of a single expense," she laughed, burying her face against his broad chest.

"What about the cost of Mike?"

"I think our first son was worth it," Michelle crooned softly in a low, throaty voice he thought the most arousing in the world.

"Me too, sweetheart," Mark spoke against the top of her gleaming hair while hugging her close.

"Would you be surprised to learn there might be a Mindy or a Marshall on the way?"

"Considering you've insisted we come to the scene of my seduction every other month since we've been married, not in the least, my darling wanton wife, not in the least!"

# Romance
# Eight

# ABOUT THE AUTHOR

## *Patricia Hagan*

### (b. 1939)

*. . . the Romance genre is special because it takes the reader into a world of fantasy . . . a world the reader wishes existed but knows that it lives only between the covers of a book.*

Patricia Hagan authored over twenty-five hundred Confession Stories before she went on to an impressive career as a novelist. She gained attention in 1972 with the publication of her first Gothic Romance, *Dark Journey Home,* followed a year later by *Winds of Terror.* Shortly afterwards, Historical Romances were becoming more and more popular, so Patricia, being commercially minded, switched genres and her great success continued.

Patricia suggests that the recent surge in popularity of Romance novels could be a reflection of the times. In other words, the stark daily routine of contemporary life can be forgotten, if only for a few hours, as the reader becomes a beautiful woman, living in an exciting, glamorous era, sought after by the most handsome men of another time. Patricia feels that a good Romance should have many happy moments as well as trials and tribulations. It should also always end on a positive note, leaving the reader completely satisfied as though she had just consumed a delightful meal. But most important, Patricia feels the reader should be made to really care about what is happening throughout the entire book.

Working four mornings a week, it takes Patricia about four months to write a 1,000 page manuscript. She works best in the morning hours, surrounded by absolute peace and quiet. To achieve this required solitude, Patricia lives in the country, where there are few distractions. She suggests that would-be writers of Romance study the craft well before beginning, and that above all they read as many books in the genre as possible, and not just their favorite author. From there on, Patricia recommends a detailed outline, hard work—and a lot of prayer!

*Works include:*

*Dark Journey Home* (1972)
*Winds of Terror* (1973)
*Love & War* (1978)
*The Raging Hearts* (1979)
*Souls Aflame* (1980)
*Love and Glory* (1982)
*Golden Roses* (1983)
*This Savage Heart* (1984)
*Love's Wine* (1985)

## *Wings of Love*

### by Patricia Hagan

and _____
*(your name here)*

A soft, gentle breeze blew across the lush, green lawn, lifting and swaying the draping weeping willow limbs into a teasing dance in the air. The silvery song of the full moon above cast eerie shadows upon the faces of the couple hidden within the umbrella of the swaying fronds.

Jillianne felt secure, if only for the moment, as Neil held her tightly against him. Cupping her face with one hand, he teased her lips lightly with his mustache before whispering, "You have only to say the word, and my heart is yours to command, my dearest. I will marry you and make you mistress of all you see before you."

Jillianne winced inwardly with pain as his lips melted against hers, and his kiss tasted of warm, sweet wine. She wanted him so desperately, knew that if she gave in to the fiery passion that was consuming the both of them, he might keep his word and make her his wife, and also mistress of Robinwood, the most elegant and prosperous plantation in all of Alabama. But that was not what she desired above all else. Oh, no. Jillianne knew she could endure the epitome of poverty, if need be, in order to be Neil Allison's wife.

Suddenly, they sprang apart at the sound of a sharp, angry voice nearby. "Neil! Oh, how could you?"

Neil's arms fell away from Jillianne, and he sprang to his feet, dashing from the hiding place to where the distraught girl stood, sobbing brokenly.

Slowly, unnoticed, Jillianne arose and slipped away into the shadows. When she was on her way home, to the shack where she lived with her widowed mother, she paused to look behind her one last time. There was no future there, for she could never marry an Allison. No, Neil's rich, prominent family would never stand for him to marry poor white trash. She turned towards the shack, towards what was her present . . . and her future. And she did not look back again.

---

*(continue story . . .)*

_____

_____

_____

_____

_____

_____

_____

_____

*(continue story . . .)*

*(continue story . . .)*

_____

_____

_____

_____

_____

_____

_____

Jillianne spoke with not only her lips but her heart as well, for she knew it to be so, that love, true love, must have wings . . . to fly away . . . and to return if it be real. "Yes, Neil, my darling, I will marry you, and I will love you forever."

# Romance Nine

# Marion Chesney

## (b. 1936)

*I find writing a book is rather like . . .*
*having a baby. You forget the pain of it*
*all once it's over and tell everyone they*
*ought to try it themselves.*

Marion Chesney, specialist in the Regency and Edwardian Romance period, has authored over thirty books, published in both America and Europe. Her works, also appearing under the well-known pen names of Jennie Tremaine, Ann Fairfax, and Helen Crampton, have received international praise for their high-spirited romance, delightfully comic scenes, and detailed descriptions of the Regency period.

Marion loves historical research. Her bookshelves are laden with Regency reference material, diaries, and belle lettres of the period. She likes to make sure her works contain no anachronisms; all details must be in place, yet Marion does not believe her readers want a history lesson. In *Quadrille*, a story taking place on the eve of the battle of Waterloo, Marion found fascination in the slang of the day, small talk, clothes, food, flowers, and especially humor. She points out that the Regency period was a time for practical jokes, outrageous puns, and heightening snobbery in British society. Oddly enough, the Regency women were no more chaste than the women of other periods. She claims they are portrayed as virgins because that's what the readers want.

Marion got her start in writing as a teenager in Glasgow, Scotland. One evening she was approached by the features editor of the *Scottish Daily Mail*, who desperately needed a reporter to cover a talent show that night. Though at the time inexperienced, Marion did not let that stop her. She took the assignment, and eventually worked her way up to become leading theater critic of the paper. Later, she went on to become chief woman reporter of the London *Daily Express*. Marion began writing Regency Romances because she had long been a fan of Jane Austen and Georgette Heyer and also because she hoped to earn enough money to send her son through private school. She felt particularly at ease with writing Regency dialogue due to her native Scottish language.

Today Marion lives with her son and her husband, Harry Scott Gibbons, also a writer and a former spy for British intelligence, in London.

## Pen names:

Helen Crampton
Ann Fairfax
Jennie Tremaine
Charlotte Ward

## Works include:

*Regency Gold* (1980)
*Lady Margery's Intrigue* (1980)
*The Constant Companion* (1980)
*Quadrille* (1981)
*My Lords, Ladies, and Marjorie* (1981)
*Love and Lady Lovelace* (1982)
*The Ghost and Lady Alice* (1982)
*The Westerby Inheritance* (1982)
*Minerva* (1983)
*The Taming of Annabelle* (1984)
*Deirdre and Desire* (1984)
*Daphne* (1984)
*Diana the Huntress* (1985)

# My Lady Cinderella

## by Marion Chesney

and _____
*(your name here)*

"Just look at you!" cried the Earl of Marksham, turning his choleric, red-veined gaze on his only daughter. "If you ain't the Friday-est-faced chit I ever did see! It's time you got married. I ain't going to have you under foot for much longer. The house ain't big enough," he raged on, waving a pudgy arm to encompass the forty-six elegant and spacious rooms which made up Marksham Court.

"You ain't a beauty like Letitia Morrison. No one expects you to catch some paragon like Lord Simon Detayne. But some man would take you if only you would make the push."

Lady Ann laid her sewing down in her lap with a little sigh and pushed back a wisp of sandy hair and looked at her father with her vague, somewhat myopic gaze.

She was used to his scenes, but this was the first time he had ever said anything about marriage. He stood there, his back to the fire, glaring at her, waiting for her reply. The gilt clock on the mantel ticked away the seconds and the snow whispered against the windowpanes.

"Why?" asked Lady Ann in her gentle voice. "We have been so comfortable until now. Why do you suddenly wish me to get married?"

"Because," said the Earl, straightening his cravat and looking down at the tops of his shiny Hessian boots, "I'm going to get married myself. So there!"

_____

*(continue story . . .)*

_____

_____

_____

*(continue story . . .)*

*(continue story . . .)*

_____

_____

_____

_____

_____

_____

_____

_____

_____

_____

The Earl of Marksham felt an unmanly lump of emotion rising in his throat and blew his nose so loudly that he quite drowned out the voices of the choir.

His daughter gave his arm a squeeze as he started to lead her down the aisle of St. George's, Hanover Square, to where her future husband, Lord Simon Detayne, stood waiting. Who would have thought, mused the Earl, that little Ann would turn out such a beauty, would take society by storm, and would win the heart of the most handsome man in London?

The Earl noticed the intense, brooding, smouldering look on the face on his future son-in-law as he gazed on his approaching bride, and, looking down, the Earl saw his daughter's face, through the delicate lace of her wedding veil, turn a delicate shade of pink.

"By George!" thought the Earl in sudden shock. "I believe they've been and gone and done it already."

Which, of course, they had.

# Romance
# Ten

# *Barbara Michaels (Barbara Mertz)*

*I am still old-fashioned; I like my hero
and heroine to be committed mentally and
emotionally and—if I may use a dirty
word—morally, before they go to bed.*

Barbara Michaels is actually the popular pen name of American writer Barbara Mertz, who has authored over thirty Romantic Suspense novels. Her first published works consisted of several nonfiction books on Egyptology, her academic specialty, in which she acquired a Ph.D. At the same time, however, Barbara found herself a devout fan of Romantic Suspense novels. As the genre rose in popularity, she decided to give it a try, and from then on she was hooked.

Barbara first began writing Gothic novels simply because those were the type of novels she herself enjoyed reading. Interestingly, Barbara appears in all of her stories in the form of her heroines, exhibiting her own personal strengths and weaknesses. In terms of her other characters, however, she never uses real people as that would conflict with her principles. Her heroines always possess intelligence and independence. If one of her characters falls into a man's arms, it is out of love and not need; they don't need men for financial or emotional support. In fact, in one of her books, the heroine turns down marriage from both suitors in favor of getting herself a job. Barbara feels that Romance novels appeal to unfulfilled yearnings of men and women because both sexes want tenderness and caring, not just physical contact. She deplores romantic fiction that continues to depict women as sex objects.

Barbara doesn't keep to a regular work schedule, preferring to work under the pressure of looming deadlines. When she does begin her work, she goes at it continually, long hours at a time, in the privacy of her study overlooking a beautiful solarium. Barbara believes that if ideas don't pop up out of the subconscious, there is no way to force them out. Her advice for the up-and-coming novelist is to *write*. She feels the way to learn to write is by doing. Her only other recommendation is to be very persistent.

Barbara, mother of two grown children, lives in a house which was built around 1820, in the Maryland woods. Neighbors say the house is haunted, but Barbara believes ghost stories exist only between the pages of a good book.

*Pen names:*

Barbara Michaels
Elizabeth Peters

*Works include:*

*Dark on the Other Side* (1977)
*Greygallows* (1977)
*Witch* (1978)
*House of Many Shadows* (1978)
*Wings of the Falcon* (1978)
*Wait for What Will Come* (1979)
*Ammie Come Home* (1979)
*Someone in the House* (1981)
*Black Rainbow* (1982)
*Here I Stay* (1983)
*Lovers Are Losers* (1984)

# Shadow of the Past

## by Barbara Michaels
### and _____
(your name here)

When the voice on the telephone told me Great-Aunt Martha was dead, I didn't say anything. I couldn't honestly say I was sorry, and common decency prevented me from saying what I really felt. After a moment of not-so-reverent silence, the voice went on to inform me that Aunt Martha had left me all her worldly goods. That was too much. I blurted out, "Who is this, really? Joel? Bob? Cut it out, that's not funny."

The lawyer didn't think it was funny either. I apologized; but I was still suspicious, till I got to his office the next day and discovered that he, at least, was real. I still couldn't believe someone wasn't playing a joke on me.

"Mr. Fredericks, Great-Aunt Martha hates—hated—my guts. I was only two when she adopted me, after my mother died. She didn't like me then, she only acted out of a sense of duty, and she made a point of mentioning that fact at least once a week for almost sixteen years. The last thing she said to me when I walked out was that she hoped I died in agony and went straight to the particular corner of hell reserved for ungrateful bastards."

Mr. Fredericks looked a trifle shaken. "She said that?"

"Well, maybe not in those exact words. I'm not illegitimate, as it happens. But in dear old Martha's eyes, my parents' marriage was never legal. You see, my father's grandmother was black."

"I see."

"Aunt Martha wouldn't leave me her old cleaning rags, much less the precious sacred family mansion in Charleston."

"Apparently she changed her mind."

"Not her."

"*Obviously* she changed her mind." Mr. Fredericks was getting impatient. He indicated the papers on his desk—Aunt Martha's will. "She has left you the house and all its contents, the only condition being that you live in the house for six months before you put it on the market. That is not unreasonable; it will take some time to dispose of the antiques and find a buyer, the condition of the market being what it is."

"I don't want the house or anything in it." I shivered, and Mr. Fredericks looked at me curiously. "Turn it over to the residuary legatee, or whatever the term is. A home for lily-white genteel daughters of the Confederacy?"

"No. Your cousin, Blakeney Talbot." He waited a minute for that to sink in. Then he added, "You would be very foolish to refuse, Miss Avery. There is a good deal of money involved. Think about it before you decide."

"I'll discuss it with my fiancé," I said. Joel would have hooted at that word; but we were planning to get married some day, when we got around to it. However, I think I had made up my mind before I left the lawyer's office. My dear cousin Blakeney . . . I had a lot of old scores to settle with Blake.

_(continue story . . .)_

*(continue story . . .)*

*(continue story . . .)*

_____

_____

_____

_____

_____

_____

_____

Gasping for breath, we dropped to the ground under the big cedar and watched the fire seize the house. _____'s bare arms were black with soot. Angry blisters were already rising on his scorched hands. We had gotten out just in time. A great gush of flame spouted from the window of an upstairs room—Aunt Martha's room. For a moment it seemed to reach out hungrily like a long groping arm, then it was lost in a flickering sheet of fire as the whole west front caught. Thunder crashed overhead. The storm would break soon, but it would come too late to save the house. Nothing could save it now, it was gone forever, along with the fiery spirit that had damned it. Good-bye, Aunt Martha, I thought, and turned my face to _____'s shoulder as his arms closed around me.

# Romance
# Eleven

# Nora Roberts (Elly Aufdem-Brinke)
## (b. 1950)

*I believe reading, more than anything else, influenced me to write. And I'll read anything from soup cans to Chaucer.*

Nora Roberts is the well-known pen name of Contemporary Romance writer Elly Aufdem-Brinke, one of Silhouette Books' most outstanding authors. To date, she has sold over fifteen manuscripts to Silhouette, including the top-selling novel *Irish Thoroughbred*, which has been translated into French, German, and Japanese. Elly is the recipient of the 1983 Romance Writers of America Award for her sensual novel *The Heart's Victory*.

As a young homemaker living with her family in an isolated Blue Ridge mountain retreat, Elly devoured scores of Romance novels to escape the constant threat of boredom. During the harsh winter months when the ultrasteep road to their home became inaccessible, baking bread and reading were her only diversions. Then, after months of shaking her head with the realization that she could write just as well as anyone, Elly decided to give it a try. After several months of writing and rewriting, she sold her first manuscript to a small Romance magazine. Everything she has written since then has been grabbed by Simon & Schuster's Silhouette.

The wide reader appeal that sets Nora Roberts apart from about 4,000 other American Romance writers may be found in the fact that her characters are always warm and her ideas unusual. For example, Elly's heroines run the gamut from stable girl to lion tamer. Though they may be young, lacking in sophistication, they are not lacking in intelligence and common sense. Elly maintains that books about people must contain human elements: temper, tenderness, and humor. But she goes on to contend that the key ingredient in a successful Romance will always be the relationship between the two lovers. Her stories contain genuine liking between her heroes and heroines, not just love and passion.

Elly considers a successful author to be one who perseveres, and points out that there hasn't been an author yet who didn't pile up a few rejection slips before making good. A grueling work schedule keeps her writing seven days a week, ten to thirteen hours a day—admittedly to keep up with her contracts. To achieve the proper atmosphere in which to work, Elly enjoys listening to soft background music, anything from Beethoven to the Top 40 rock. And though she considers a quiet environment ideal for writing, she seldom finds it at home. With two young children scampering about, periods of silence are few and far between.

Elly currently lives with her two boys, Dan and Jason, in her modest home atop a steep mountain lane near the Antietam Battlefield in Maryland.

*Pen names:*

Jill March
Nora Roberts

*Works include:*

*Irish Thoroughbred* (1981)
*Blithe Images* (1982)
*Search for Love* (1982)
*Island of Flowers* (1982)
*The Heart's Victory* (1982)
*Tonight and Always* (1983)

# Boundary Lines

by Nora Roberts

and _____

*(your name here)*

The wind whipped against her cheeks. It flowed, smelling faintly of spring and growing things, as it streamed through her thick mane of hair. Jillian lifted her face to it, as much in challenge as appreciation. Beneath her, the sleek mare strained for more speed. They'd ride, two free spirits, as long as the sun stayed high. Short, tough grass was crushed under hooves, along with stray wildflowers. Trees were few, but Jillian wasn't looking for the comfort of shade. As far as she could see, the land stretched. Her land. It was rolling and rich with the first of the season's wheat. A gold, undulating ocean of grain flowed on either side of her as she streaked down the worn path. Her brilliant emerald eyes took it in before she tossed back her head, sending her fiery hair bouncing.

The mare scented the water from the pond, and Jillian let her have her head. The thought of stripping off her sweaty clothes and diving in appealed to her mood. Spotting the glistening water, she urged more speed from her horse. But the mare scented something else and suddenly reared. Before Jillian could draw in a breath, she was hurtling through space. With a resounding splash, she landed bottom first in the pond.

Sputtering and furious, she wiped her wet hair from her eyes to glare at the man astride a buckskin stallion. He didn't need to have his feet on the ground for her to see that he was tall. His hair was dark, as confused by the wind as hers had been, around a face that was rawboned, weathered and roughly handsome. Jillian didn't take the time to admire the way he sat the stallion—with a casual sort of control that exuded confidence and power. What she did see was that his eyes were nearly as black as his hair. And they were laughing.

Narrowing her own, she spat at him, "What the hell are you doing on my land?"

*(continue story . . .)*

*(continue story . . .)*

Jillian turned her back on him, refusing to give way, refusing the need to feel his arms around her. "So you came back."

Aaron grinned, hooking his hands in his belt. "Did you think I wouldn't?"

A negligent shrug accompanied her words. "I didn't think about it at all."

With a speed at odds with his lazy manner, Aaron spun her around, yanking her into his arms. Jillian's chin flew up, as he had known it would. "Didn't you?" he countered. "Did you think about this?" Swiftly, his mouth rushed down to hers. As always, the moment of contact was electric, all consuming. Jillian's response was turbulent and demanding as their bodies fit unerringly together. Their lips clung, then parted, just enough for their eyes to meet.

"I hate you," she whispered as her arms circled his neck. "I hate, loathe and despise you."

"Yeah." His eyes mirrored the laughter in hers. "Me too."

# Romance
# Twelve

# ABOUT THE AUTHOR

## *Lena Kennedy*

### (b. 1914)

*Writing is the easiest hobby in the world,*
*if you've got the inclination for it.*
*All you need is a paper and pencil.*

At the age of sixty-five, a dream came true for British-born Lena Kennedy. Through a remarkable set of circumstances her first novel, *Maggie*, was published. Lena's life has been a strenuous one, with poverty and ill health making themselves no strangers to her family. During the war years she lived through loneliness, shortages, and the London bombings. But through it all she was sustained by a dream: to be a writer.

For years Lena wrote in her diary and created short stories, until she finally decided to try a novel. In 1969, she finished what was to be *Maggie*, but she didn't know how to get it published. In her ignorance, she looked in the telephone directory under "Publisher" and sent the erractically typed and misspelled manuscript off to likely sounding names (one of which turned out to be a comic book publisher). A music publisher read *Maggie* and was so impressed, he passed it on to a journalist friend. The journalist agreed with his assessment, but there the matter stopped for a while. The manuscript had been left with no address or phone number and they were unable to track Lena down. However, they accidentally found her in London's East End and assured her that the manuscript should be published. They passed the book

KATE OF CLYVE SHORE

along to England's Paddington Press and at long last, *Maggie* was published in both England and the United States. American Romance readers welcomed Lena Kennedy with open arms, making *Maggie* the "sleeper" best-seller of the year with over 800,000 copies in print! Paddington Press soon discovered that Lena had several other completed manuscripts hidden away. *Kitty* was one destined for great success. Another, *Autumn Alley*, quickly rocketed to British best-seller lists.

Success hasn't changed Lena, who still thinks up her stories while dusting and vacuuming. She lives in London's East End and spends her holidays in Kent on the property that she and her husband bought twenty-five years ago.

*Works include:*

*Maggie* (1980)
*Kitty* (1981)
*Autumn Alley* (1981)
*Nely Kely* (1982)
*Lizzie* (1983)
*Lady Penelope* (1983)
*Susan* (1984)
*Dandelion Seed* (1984)

# *Kate of Clyve Shore*

### by Lena Kennedy

and _____
(your name here)

The more Kate thought about becoming a fine lady, the more discontent her expression grew. Her bottom lip drooped until it resembled one of those luscious ripe strawberries that grew in the fields of Kent. Kate was a most unusual looking girl. Her face grew wide at the brow and narrowed at the chin. Her long black hair lay flat on her forehead and fell to her waist in two thick braids. The most outstanding feature of her face was her beautiful eyes. They were deep set and dark blue, the colour of a calm sea. At the time of our story she was just turned fifteen years old, a sweet slow-witted girl, a yeoman's daughter, brought up in that small village of Kent. She lived all her life in that tiny cottage out on the marsh in sight of the huge castle where the majority of the inhabitants of Clyve Shore obtained a livelihood. She had trudged back and forth along that dry sandy road leading to the castle for as long as she could remember, carrying a heavy linen basket on her head. She stepped out very briskly on her long beautiful legs, her back as straight as a soldier's. The basket contained the frills and furbelows of the gentry staying at the castle, white ruffs to wear about the neck and lace frills to be attached to the cuffs. Kate's mother washed, boiled, starched and ironed endlessly day after day, until the walls of the little cottage ran with steam. Her mother had been a servant at the castle in her youth as had generations of her family before her, ever since the time of the Norman occupation from which Kate had inherited her small hooked nose and acquired the name of De Faunce.

Every day as she walked along the winding road she dreamed her fanciful dreams. Such beautiful scenery surrounded her . . . the green flat rolling marshland leading down to the Thames on one side of the road, and on the other a dense forest of magnificent trees. But Kate was oblivious to all this beauty as she walked along in the golden sunshine. She was too busy daydreaming. One day she would find a rich husband who would buy her fine clothes and take her mother and young brother away from that damp steamy cottage that worsened her mother's cough. Pa could stay where he was, serving that old priest he was so fond of. . . . Perhaps that would teach him not to call her daft, saying she was always dreaming, walking along with her mouth open as though catching flies—cheeky old devil. As she neared the end of her journey, her mind was made up. The first fine gentleman who asked her hand in marriage, she would accept. . . .

*(continue story . . .)*

*(continue story . . .)*

_____

_____

_____

_____

_____

_____

_____

_____

_____

_____

_____

_____

_____

_____

_____

_____

_____

_____

_____

_____

*(continue story . . .)*

With a final groan, the old oak tree gave up, keeled over and crashed down onto the body of Katey. Her spirit soared up over the marsh to join that of her ancestors. Tom walked in the cold dawn still calling "Katey my love, where are you? Please answer me." He covered ten miles of wasteland before he found her. The next day Kate was buried in a small corner of Clyve churchyard. There was no priest available as he had fled from the fire. Richard Little had ridden over with help for the stricken families and he read the burial service. After the service Tom sat for a long time outside on the church wall. While sitting and thinking, he whittled a bust of Katey, an exact replica of her, wide full mouth, heart-shaped face and mane of hair, tight under a little cap. When it was finished, he laid it on the newly turned earth, "That's all I have to give you, Katey; my heart is with it," he murmured. Then he turned sharply and left the churchyard to join the band of followers who waited for him. They slowly made their way to the next house and in time Tom gained favour as a preacher. To the memory of Katey is the sweet carved bust; it is posed on a windowsill inside the church and no one knows who put it there.

# Romance
# Thirteen

# V. C. Andrews

## (b. 1943)

> *. . . let your imagination flow. Don't inhibit it with thoughts of what your mother will think when she reads what you write. Write all the things you've always wished other authors would include in their Romances.*

Dubbed "the fastest-selling author in the United States" by *The New York Times*, V. C. (Virginia Cleo) Andrews has become one of the publishing industry's most phenomenal success stories. She is the author of the enormously popular *Flowers in the Attic*, *Petals on the Wind*, *If There Be Thorns*, and, fourth in her series of thrillers, *My Sweet Audrina*. All shot to the heights of best-seller lists nationwide, with each boasting in-print figures in the millions. Though not typically an author of the Romance genre, Virginia has recently become very much intrigued by it. She concedes that one day she may· *complete* a Romance herself—especially now that she's got "the feel," having written *Love's Savage Desire* for *Your First Romance*.

Virginia believes that stories are everywhere to be found in our lives. She keeps her ideas fresh and invigorating by piecing together bits from her own life and the lives of others and, of course, inventing a little as well. Virginia enjoys giving her characters free rein to do as they please. She insists on letting them take over their own stories, at times surprising even her. Virginia suggests new writers keep their characters constantly thwarted, frustrated, and in trouble throughout a novel; never let up until the story's end.

A first draft, containing some dialogue and description, can be written by Virginia in as little as four hours; she prefers this technique to an outline. A completed book can take her anywhere from five months to a year, depending on how well she knows her characters. She will not tolerate radio or television (except the news) while working, and when real creativity strikes, she works for long solitary hours without interruption. Virginia feels that beginning writers must never write the kind of books they themselves would not enjoy reading. Once having decided upon a specific genre, she advises them to read as much as possible within it, take notes on story transitions, and summarize plots. This, she says, will give beginning writers a feel of how a novel is put together.

Virginia has been written up in such national publications as *Family Circle*, *People*, and *The New York Times*. She currently lives in her home state of Virginia, where she enjoys backgammon, bridge, and classical music.

## *Works include:*

*Flowers in the Attic* (1979)
*Petals on the Wind* (1980)
*If There Be Thorns* (1981)
*My Sweet Audrina* (1982)
*The Seeds of Yesterday* (1984)

# *Love's Savage Desire*

### by V. C. Andrews

and _____
*(your name here)*

There wasn't a light to be seen, no farmlands were tilled and ready for spring planting. Peering through the window of the carriage which careened drunkenly over the rocky and rutted dirt road heading obviously for that highest mountain with the dark castle riding its top, Taretta Llewellyn sought some other sign of human inhabitation. It was then she heard the lonely and somehow frightening wail of an animal, not quite wolf or dog.

Troubled thoughts ran through her head. Who was this man who claimed to be her father's uncle—when she knew her father had been an only child? Had it been a mistake to lie and tell the authorities she did remember an uncle? Why had he sent for her? And would that high and forbidding castle be a better home than the misery of the orphanage she'd just escaped?

An hour later she was standing before a massive wooden door that was barred across with iron. The night was bitterly cold. The wind whipped her raven tresses free of her bonnet. Her thin clothes felt inadequate as she waited for someone to respond to the driver's urgent pounding. Resting beside her feet was her single bag, containing all the pitiful possessions she'd managed to acquire in her seventeen years. Her heart pounded madly with the expectation of seeing someone like her father when the door opened. But when it did, the man who stood there sent a terrifying shiver down her spine. Her lips parted to sound a scream that she quickly smothered.

*(continue story . . .)*

_____

_____

_____

_____

*(continue story . . .)*

*(continue story . . .)*

_____

_____

_____

_____

_____

_____

_____

_____

On the highest rampart of the castle, Tara stared toward the west from which he'd come—if he still lived. She'd been seventeen when first she met him, and had almost screamed when she beheld him. In his castle she'd found terror beyond belief, and love beyond her expectations. And if given the option to live again through the terror, she would ten times over again, if only she knew he lived. Hour after hour she waited there, the wind whipping her dark locks until the failing day left only a hint of promised dawn in the coming night. I'll forgive him everything, she thought, forgive him anything, if only he comes back to me. But when the moon was riding high, she was on her knees still praying, bowed down with grief . . . for he'd be back before dark, if he still lived. Then, as she sagged, all hopes gone, she heard again that lonely, heart-wrenching wail of an animal not dog or wolf. Coming over the hills toward home . . . he was coming back. "I'm coming, Tara," she thought she heard him cry, but she was up and running to meet him halfway, ready and eager to be crushed this time in his arms, and this time her lips would be just as savagely demanding as his.

# Romance
# Fourteen

# ABOUT THE AUTHOR

## *Barbara Riefe* (*Alan Riefe*)
### (b. 1925)

*You'll find there's nothing in this world to equal the satisfaction of accomplishment in turning out a saleable novel.*

Barbara Riefe is the pen name of Alan Riefe, who, in addition to his popular Romances, has authored a series of Westerns. Born the son of missionary parents in Tientsin, China, Alan Riefe moved to New Zealand before coming to settle in the United States. He began writing magazine articles in his late teens, and in 1976 sold his premiere Romance, *This Ravaged Heart*, first of the Dandridge Trilogy. Currently in its eighth printing, the success of *This Ravaged Heart* has initiated a rippling effect of eleven Barbara Riefe Romances, which have appeared on seventeen best-seller lists, including *The New York Times'*.

Alan's Romance novels had strictly been Historical until 1981, the year that marked his first departure from the nineteenth century and into the waiting arms of the twentieth, with his trilogy, the Shackleford Legacy. Alan recognizes that his works provide a necessary escape for his readers. A Historical Romance, he contends, should not have to depend on historical incident to hold the reader, but rather upon an original, highly imaginative story which uses only that point in time as a springboard.

To the beginning writers of Romance, Alan suggests a fine-tooth study of the books they themselves enjoy. Also, the plot should come out of the characters, the characters must be consistent, the plot twists acceptable, and so on. But most important, he feels one has to work, work, work. And for Alan, peace and quiet are all he requires to do just that. Alan is married and the father of three children.

*Pen name:*

Barbara Riefe

*Works include:*

*This Ravaged Heart* (1976)
*Far Beyond Desire* (1977)
*Fire and Flesh* (1977)
*So Wicked the Heart* (1979)
*Wild Fire* (1980)
The Shackleford Legacy (1981–82)
*An Extraordinary Woman* (1983)
*The Loves of Alexandra* (1983)
*Wicked Fire* (1983)

# *Bold Passion's Price*

## by Barbara Riefe

and_____
*(your name here)*

The morning had broken clear and sweltering, the tropical sun focusing its fury on the *Benjamin,* lying at anchor off the northeast tip of the island of Hawaii, so close that Samantha, standing at the rail, could see the forbidding shoreline under assault by waterfalls, plunging down the sheer cliffs into the turquoise sea. Crowning the cliffs, the land angled sharply upward, reaching a wide band of lush green growth that climbed to the tree line, which in turn rose to the volcanoes, Mauna Loa and Mauna Kea.

The fever had so weakened her she had to lean on the rail for support. She should not be out of bed, she knew, but the cabin was stifling, the air unbreathable; at least here on deck should an offshore breeze spring up, she could enjoy it. Jason would be furious with her; to be married to a doctor had its drawbacks as well as its obvious advantages. Whenever she fell ill even in the slightest, he all but suffocated her with attention, hovering over her, alternately dosing and purging her, treating her like a prematurely born child whose life hung by a slender thread. He was ashore now with Captain Kirkland, the young, black-bearded master of the *Benjamin,* whose fierce eyes never met hers without betraying undisguisable lust; his leering grin directed at her invariably sent a tremor of revulsion across her shoulders. An extraordinarily capable seaman, in Jason's opinion, but a cruel man, harsh and relentless, who only two days earlier had broken his bosun's jaw for "gross insubordination." With her master ashore, the *Benjamin* had been left in charge of Orrin Cain, the first mate, a dark-eyed, dark-haired man with strikingly handsome features and on sight the most sensuous man Samantha had ever met.

She peered under her hand, searching for the long boat, but it was lost in the green foliage which came down to meet the sea. All at once she sensed that someone was standing behind her. Slowly, she turned her head. It was Orrin Cain, stripped to the waist, muscles rippling beneath his deeply tanned arms and massive chest. He smiled, touching the peak of his cap in greeting.

"Morning, ma'am, feeling better?"

*(continue story . . .)*

*(continue story . . .)*

*(continue story . . .)*

_____

_____

_____

_____

_____

_____

_____

_____

His chest crushed her breasts, but she uttered no word of protest, reveling in the pressure and tightening her grip around his neck. She had waited so patiently so long for this meeting of flesh, this divine and delicious contact. The world and time that had separated them for so insufferably long dissolved, yielding to the moment. Now at last he was hers; the sweet substance of anticipation, the bridled passions, the torturous yearning were all in the past now, banished to memory. His swollen tongue in fierce and slippery combat with her own fired her senses and she shivered, her thighs trembling as his throbbing manhood thrust slowly forward between them, reaching her sex, encroaching, entering, filling her. He moved within her and she gasped and moaned, driving her hips upward, engorging him. Through the maelstrom of ecstasy that engulfed her in capitulation there crept a single discernible impression, conscious relief that the hell on earth that had been her life in captivity was gone forever.

She was free and safe at last, protected by a love that would endure forever.

# Romance Fifteen

# ABOUT THE AUTHOR

## *Virginia Coffman*
### (b. 1914)

*Oddly enough, I couldn't write
while undergoing a particularly
tormenting love affair. But
what fun afterwards. Putting
the rat in a book. In fact,
at least 15 books.*

Ever since Virginia Coffman saw the silent movie *Ben Hur* on October 16, 1927, she knew that she wanted to write historical novels for the rest of her life. After twenty-five years of persistent writing, Virginia sold her first novel, *Maura*. It combined the typical ingredients of the nineteenth-century Gothic, and became a major success. To Virginia, background is foremost in the creation of her works. She is considered an expert on various periods of history, primarily the French Revolution and Ancient Rome. She has written over sixty-five novels and has sold more than seven million copies in America and Europe.

A reasonable plot and a realistic heroine, such as Scarlett O'Hara in *Gone with the Wind*, are key factors in writing a successful Romance, according to Virginia. In the development of her characters, she borrows bits, pieces, traits, ambitions, and individual quirks from people she has known; notably a former lover, as well as her father, who appears as either hero or villain in several of her books.

Virginia's advice to the budding Romance writer is simple—write what you like to read, study the markets, and write something every day, whether good or bad. Virginia writes five pages a day, seven days a week. Having no husband or children to distract her, the only competition for her attention are the daily episodes of "General Hospital," "One Life to Live," and "The Edge of Night," which serve to keep her company while she writes.

*Pen name:*

Kay Cameron
Jeanne Duval
Anne Stanfield

*Works include:*

*Maura* (1959)
*Veronique* (1976)
*The Gaynor Women* (1978)
*The Ravishers* (1980, as Jeanne Duval)
*Pacific Cavalcade* (1981)
*Lumbard Cavalcade* (1982)
*Lumbard Heiress* (1983)
*The Orchid Tree* (1984)
*Lord of the Moors* (1984)
*Passion's Rebel* (1984, as Kay Cameron)

# *Yankee Duchess*

## by Virginia Coffman

and_____
*(your name here)*

"But why me?" Maryl asked, with reason. There must be a dozen secretaries in the mayor's office with more seniority. And you didn't become a reigning grand duke's dinner partner every day.

"Because, honey, our esteemed mayor's wife has a gallstone attack, and can't make the reception. We've got about an hour for the switch. Frankly, you're the only dame in this office that she doesn't think is after that little tub of a husband of hers."

"Look, Si, I haven't a thing that would be appropriate for a ding like this."

"Go buy something. Within reason. But do it in the next ten minutes."

My God! she thought. Somebody's going to give me one good pinch and I'll wake up. . . . She was remembering Grand-Duke Christian-Frederik on the six o'clock news last night. A casting director's delight. Tall, dark, handsome, eligible, and oozing with charm. . . .

"Okay. I'll suffer through it. If you insist. But I'll want portal-to-portal pay."

*(continue story . . .)*

_____

_____

_____

_____

_____

_____

*(continue story . . .)*

*(continue story . . .)*

 

Colonel Stefan's smile was a trifle grim. It gave his sensuous mouth a hard reminder of her first meeting with him. "I don't imagine His Grace will want to see me again." He saluted and then looked into her eyes. What he saw gave the Slavic curve of his own eyes a glow of warmth. He took her hand into his palm, holding it tightly. He drew her to him. His lips stifled any protest she might have made. Engrossed in that kiss, she was hardly aware of the throat clearing behind her, and the ironic comment of His Grace, Christian-Frederik:

"I take it that there will be a slight recasting of the groom's role at the cathedral this afternoon."

# Romance
# Sixteen

# *Barbara Bonham*

## (b. 1926)

*Women are inherently romantic. . . . Most
novels contain a love story, but only in
the Romance genre can a woman find the pure
article. Reading Romances not only lets
her experience romance, it offers escape
from the stresses of her life, and here,
unlike life, she is always assured of a
happy ending.*

At the age of twenty-one, Barbara Bonham enrolled in a correspondence
course in writing. Three years later she sold her first story. Though she does
not credit the course for her early success, she admits that it did at least get her
started. Barbara began her career by writing Confession Stories, but soon her
interest in pioneer history took charge. She wrote a number of books with
historical backgrounds for children aged ten to fourteen. She also wrote three
nurse novels and a Gothic, *Sweet and Bitter Fancy.*

Knowing Barbara's fascination with history, her agent advised her to try
Historical Romance, since at the time it was a new and growing market.
Hence Barbara wrote *Proud Passion*—the story of a beautiful and brave woman
who comes from France to find love and adventure in the savage frontier
wilderness of the Ohio River country. It was published in 1976 by Playboy
Press as their first Historical Romance. This was followed by the successful
*Passion's Price*, which made *The New York Times* best-seller list.

Barbara's books are carefully researched. She values old newspapers as a
perfect source to get the feel of a period or place. She strives to understand
what an ordinary day in an ordinary life was like. She recognizes that readers

are interested in people, in what happens to them, in their problems and how they are solved. With that in mind, her novels promise to transport the reader into another world, paying careful attention to many details, such as the costume of the period.

According to Barbara, writing is the only way one learns to write; the more one writes, the better craftsman one becomes. Her own schedule demands she write 1,000 to 2,000 words in a five-hour day. She prefers to write in longhand due to her dislike of typewriters. Solitude and quiet are essentials to Barbara's creative environment, but physical quiet alone is not enough—her mind and emotions must also be at peace. Barbara lives in her home state of Nebraska with her husband, Max.

*Pen name:*

Sara North

*Works include:*

*Sweet and Bitter Fancy* (1976)
*Proud Passion* (1976)
*Passion's Price* (1977)
*Dance of Desire* (1978)
*Jasmine for My Grave* (1978, as Sara North)
*Dark Side of Passion* (1980)
*Green Willow* (1982)
*Bittersweet* (1984)

# Love Wears Only One Face

## by Barbara Bonham

and_____
*(your name here)*

The hall swirled with color and gaiety. Nara sat apart from it, her hands clenched in her lap, a smile pasted on her face. It should have been she wearing that bridal gown, she who had stood beside Doane and received his vow to love and cherish her until death parted them. How could he have done this to her? He had loved her, she was sure of it. He couldn't have been pretending all those times when they had met in their secret place and made love. Even now she could hear the special way he always told her he loved her. Closing her eyes, she could feel his strong warm hands teasing her body, his kisses building a fire in her blood until finally she was gasping, "Please, please."

A hungry shudder went through her and she opened her eyes swiftly, creating the smile again, looking as if she were enjoying herself. Across the room Doane stood tall and graceful beside his bride, his dark head bent to catch something she was saying. It was something intimate despite the fact that they were surrounded by well-wishers; Nara sensed it even at this distance. Just for an instant, she closed her eyes again. When she opened them, Doane was coming toward her. His eyes held hers; her heart jumped to her throat. As he drew near her, he said in a voice no one else could hear, "Meet me at midnight in our special place."

"But you're—"

"Meet me!" he demanded urgently and passed on by.

_____
*(continue story . . .)*
_____

_____

*(continue story . . .)*

*(continue story . . .)*

_____

_____

_____

_____

_____

_____

_____

_____

_____

_____

_____

_____

_____

She gave a final brush to her hair and got into bed, piling pillows behind her back, pulling a long tress of blonde hair over one shoulder the way he liked it, retying the ribbon at the neck of her gown. Then she waited with fast beating heart. The journey to this moment had been a long painful one, but it had taught her a precious lesson. Love wore only one face. All others were masks. The bedroom door opened, revealing the face of her love; smiling, he came toward her. She opened her arms to him and brought him home.

# Romance

# Seventeen

# *Malcolm Macdonald*

## (b. 1932)

*. . . a great Romance is like*
*beauty that needs no cosmetic.*

When Malcolm Macdonald, British author, historian, illustrator, and country squire, began writing Romances, he set out to become the very opposite of what the word "novelist" had come to mean. Rather, Malcolm preferred to be known as a simple storyteller. His stories are heavily influenced by thirteen years as a nonfiction writer when he made a living writing medical books, guidebooks, and books on wildlife.

Malcolm exhibits a preoccupation with facts in his works, due to an obsession with history. Though his plots and characters are all invented, the historical facts in his novels are certain to be authentic. The large collection of Victorian source books, textbooks, topographies, and autobiographies he collects offer him a deep reservoir of information from which he draws story material.

Malcolm writes Romance for the reader. His goals are to entertain and enthrall. The reader of Romance, according to Malcolm, seems to enjoy such basic themes as heterosexual love, money making/losing, family love and tensions, bringing up children, conflict between generations, and fortune— both good and bad. These are the topics he believes most occupy people's lives. For Malcolm, all good stories have the same key ingredients: a spellbinding plot; strong, well-mixed characters; interesting locations; and suspension of disbelief. He finds special fascination in thrusting his characters into situations or challenges for which they are untrained, then watching to see where they find the strength and courage to cope with them.

Malcolm writes nearly every day from nine o'clock in the morning to midnight. And, of course, when he's not writing, he's thinking of his writing. His thoughts for beginning writers are plain and simple—writing must be done especially when the mind is blank, and if after ten minutes there are still no words on the page, another career should be considered.

Malcolm lives with his wife, Ingrid, in his secluded fifteen-acre country house, ninety miles outside of Dublin, Ireland. He is the father of two daughters, and dearly loves the country and horse riding.

*Pen names:*

Malcolm Ross
Malcolm Ross-Macdonald

*Works include:*

*The World from Rough Stones* (1974)
*The Rich Are with You Always* (1976)
*Sons of Fortune* (1978)
*Abigail* (1979)
*The Dukes* (1981, as Malcolm Ross)
*Goldeneye* (1981)
*Tessa d'Arblay* (1983)
*In Love and War* (1984)

# The Panther Feast

## by Malcolm Macdonald
### and_____
*(your name here)*

The moment she saw the cottage it whispered "home!" to her—though she had never set eyes on it, indeed, had never been in this locality, in her life.

The pony and trap had come half a mile down the little railway station, up a winding, leafy land toward the village. At the junction with the main road stood the pretty little Victorian cottage. "Home," it whispered again.

It was so exactly what Jessica had hoped to find when she set out to rebuild her shattered life that for a moment she could only sit and stare. In the drowsy summer heat the pony walked at a snail's pace, so she had all the time in the world to notice that the windows were uncurtained and the garden was overrun with weeds. The place cried out for love and care—exactly the sort of love and care she suddenly longed to give it. Houses weren't like people. Houses didn't die. You'd never have to walk away from the grave of a house wondering what you were going to do with the next fifty years of emptiness.

"That cottage," she said to the driver. "Who owns it?"

The fellow turned, stared at it, looked at her, and then spat viciously upon the road. It was such an extraordinary response from a man who until then had been so pleasant that she didn't know what to say. Then he pointed toward the roadside, where now there reared a long, high wall of warm-coloured Cotswold stone. It was many centuries older than the cottage and was obviously the boundary of some great country estate. "Him," he said. "Him in there. Sir Jethro. God's curse on him!"

His grim tone darkened the afternoon; the trees, which were all she could see above the wall, now seemed forbidding and sinister where before they had been graceful and summery. She stole a last glimpse at the cottage, mellow and tranquil in the sun; it, at least, still seemed a haven of peace.

In a short while they turned a corner and passed an imposing pair of entrance gates. A cedar-lined drive curved lazily uphill through manicured parkland to a jewel of a mansion—part Tudor, part classical. It could only be the home of this Sir Jethro, whom the driver detested so heartily, but who was also the owner of the only thing she now wanted in all the world. On an impulse she said, "I've changed my mind. Take me up there."

"That I will not!" the man answered immediately.

"Please. I want to meet this Sir Jethro. I want to rent that cottage we saw back there." When he failed to respond, she added, "Look—I don't want to go on into the village."

The man reined the pony to a halt. Slowly and without a word, he descended to the road. He took off her bag and set it down in the dust.

"What's this?" she asked.

"You could pay me a thousand pounds, and it'd still get you no nearer to Marton Hall than you are now." He held out a hand to help her descend.

She spurned it angrily and leaped down unaided. "Very well," she said, her eyes bright with anger. "I shall walk."

The driver shrugged and remounted his seat. "Don't you never say you wasn't warned," he shouted back at her as the trap moved slowly away. "For I tell you now—you go up there . . . you get mixed up with that devil, and you'll spend the rest of your life wishing you'd never got down off this here cart."

_(continue story . . .)_

_____

_____

_____

_____

_____

_____

_____

_____

*(continue story . . .)*

*(continue story . . .)*

_____

_____

_____

_____

_____

_____

_____

_____

She heard the deep crunch of the Rolls on the gravel of the carriage sweep and ran downstairs. Jethro was already standing in the hall. He looked at her, at the house, at everything, without recognition.

"You weren't long," she said.

He made a strange noise. For a moment she thought it was a sob, but it was only the sudden inhalation of a man too bewildered to remember to breathe. "It doesn't take long to ruin a man," he said flatly.

She paused, waiting for some sign of his true mood; this calm was so unlike him.

"They've taken everything," he went on in that same lost, straying voice. "We're left with nothing."

Still his lack of passion marooned her at the foot of the stairs. "Oh, darling . . . ," she prompted.

He looked at her then. An odd smile twitched at the corners of his mouth. She realized her own lips were wide open; her tongue was dry. He chuckled. There was a sudden warmth in him, such as she had not known since the first year of their marriage—though why should she think of that now, after all that had happened between them!

"Bloody fools!" he said. "They think they've beaten me. They don't realize they've left me the only thing of any value in my entire life."

Awkwardly he began to raise his arms toward her and all at once she understood what he was trying to say.

It tore her apart. One half of her wanted to spare him the humiliation of this confession and apology, wanted to rush into his arms, hold him tight, tell him not to worry. But she had stumbled down that route too many times to take it so easily now. The other, wiser half told her Jethro had to go through this ordeal; he had to earn back the love she was so willing to shower upon him—or he would never truly value it.

So, with an exulting heart and the joy rising in her like a starburst, she stood her ground and forced him through every grovelling syllable. Some of it was prepared, but she didn't mind that; at least it showed he had been thinking about him and her.

She almost left her own response too late—until he was forced to say, "Of course, I realize I can't possibly expect you to share such a future with me. If you want . . . to . . . to go your own way, I'll quite understand."

"Oh darling!" Her joy erupted suddenly. "Do you really mean that? Really and really and truly?"

A terrible pain came into his eyes. With horror she saw that he completely misunderstood her happiness—he thought she was overjoyed at the prospect of separating from him. That old, hard edge came back into his voice as he turned toward the morning room. "Goodbody shall draw up the papers tomorrow."

His angry tread made such a clatter on the marble that he failed to hear her running up behind him until she was almost at his elbow. He half turned. She ran full tilt into him, bearing him back against the wainscot. He stumbled and slipped over. She fell with him. A tall jardiniere on an elegant wooden stand teetered and fell, missing him by inches. It made a mighty crash.

He sprawled among the strewn earth, on the marble floor, among the shattered porcelain, gasping with astonishment. She lay upon him, clinging to him, laughing and laughing until the breath left her body. He hugged her, experimentally at first and then with all his old fire and passion.

As ancient fires rekindled, the solemnity of this moment claimed them both. "If you want to know the truth—I'm glad it happened," he murmured into the furnace of her ear. He drew breath to say more, but no words came.

Between them was no further need of words.

# Romance
# Eighteen

# ABOUT THE AUTHOR

## Roberta Gellis

### (b. 1927)

*I don't consider myself a writer.*
*I'm a storyteller. I tell a story*
*in words as natural as I can find.*
*It's as if I'm speaking to the reader.*

Medieval specialist Roberta Gellis was born into a family of great achievers. Her mother was a Greek and Latin scholar, and her father a well-known chemist. Thus, it was quite natural that she develop dual interests in science and historical literature. First earning a B.S. in chemistry, then an M.S. in biochemistry, Roberta went on to achieve an M.A. for her studies in medieval literature. Creator of the popular Roselynde Chronicles, today she is one of the most distinguished authors of Historical Romances.

Roberta is meticulous in her research. Her Historical Romances are renowned for their accuracy of time, place, and event. Her plots are determined by the historical events she is describing and although most of her heroes and heroines are fictitious, everyone around them is quite genuine. Her special strength lies in the type of heroines she creates. They are strong but enchanting; they dominate, but they are also tender and full of understanding. She believes the most important factor in creating a great Romance is the development of real human characters with real human problems who find real human solutions. The underlying theme evident in her work is a belief that all people in all times have needed love, and that this affects a person's response to and vision of the events the person lives through.

Like most writers, Roberta finds she does her best work in relative quiet, with all her research material at hand. However, she is also able to work quite well on buses and trains, in restaurants, and while her family watches television. Roberta considers herself a slow writer. She produces four to seven pages a day; it takes her about six months to complete a novel, not including time spent on research. Many times she will begin research on her next book while still writing a current work. She relies more on the journals of the day than on recent histories. Roberta rarely reads historical Romances because of a fear of subliminal plagiarism.

Roberta's advice to beginning Romance writers is the same as her advice to any other beginning writer: You've just got to sit down and do it! Roberta lives with her husband, Charles, their rambunctious Airedale, Brandy, and a brand new word processor in Roslyn Heights, New York.

*Pen names:*

Max Daniels
Priscilla Hamilton

*Works include:*

*Bond of Blood* (1976)
*Knight's Honor* (1976)
*The Dragon and the Rose* (1977)
*The Sword and the Swan* (1977)
*The English Heiress* (1980)
*The Cornish Heiress* (1981)
*The Kent Heiress* (1982)
*The Indian Heiress* (1983)
The Roselynde Chronicles (1978–1983)
The Royal Dynasty Series (1981 to present)

# Disobedient Daughter

## by Roberta Gellis

and_____
*(your name here)*

The sun, no very common guest that wet spring, looked in boldly on April 2, 1512, bringing the arms of Maryes vividly alive in the window. A steak of blood red from the chevron separating the three black hound's heads fell both upon the rich black velvet of Thomas Maryes' doublet and upon the silvery silk sleeve of Lady Maryes' gown. The crimson band linked them together, reinforcing their unity, and, indeed, their faces held similar expressions as they looked at their eldest daughter, Anne.

"I have done what I can with her, Thomas, the rest is up to you." Elizabeth Maryes' voice was calm, but it held a note of doubt, which her husband's eyes mirrored. He nodded at her, although his eyes never left the girl before him.

"She will be in good hands," he said. "The Archduchess Margaret is both kind and very lively."

"I hope she is also patient."

Sir Thomas made no direct reply to his wife's remark, but his keen eye caught the flush of color that rose under Anne's delicate skin, and he was gratified by her prettiness. "You have said nothing, Anne. Do you understand what I have planned for you?"

"Yes, father." The girl's voice was soft, a trifle breathless, and the hazel eyes she lifted to her father's face were filled with fear.

If Thomas Maryes had been given to useless gestures, he would have scratched his head in puzzlement; if he had been given to venting frustration or irritation in violence, he would have slapped his daughter's face. Instead, he shrugged cynically and laughed. To the best of his knowledge neither he nor Elizabeth had ever given Anne any cause to fear them. Indeed, he could never remember striking her; he could hardly remember speaking a harsh word to her. True, Anne had scarcely ever deserved a reprimand, being a model of propriety and docility—and there lay the rub. How had a daughter engendered by him upon Elizabeth Bassett come to be such a sop of milk and water?

*(continue story . . .)*

*(continue story . . .)*

Anne could scarcely breathe in her husband's fierce embrace, but she would not have protested if he had cracked her ribs. When he had told her he would go to Maryes Manor personally to invite her parents to their son's christening, the fragile happiness she had built so tentatively during these two years of marriage seemed about to splinter into unmendable shards. Now she realized that Peter had humbled himself only because he thought a reconciliation would make *her* happy. The bitterness in his voice when he told her they would not come, that they had not forgiven her, contrasted with the passion of his kisses, the tightness of his arms around her—as if he strove by his warmth to protect her from their coldness and indifference. Anne knew now, finally, once and for all time, that Peter had not married her for what he could gain, but because he loved her. Her joy was fragile no longer. It was built of stone as solid as Netherly's walls. It was forever.

# Romance
# Nineteen

# *Cynthia Wright*

## (b. 1953)

*The breakthrough came when Woodiwiss and
Rosemary Rogers opened the bedroom door
and we readers raced in to find out
exactly what men like Rhett Butler did
after they carried women like Scarlett
up the stairs!*

Cynthia Wright sold her first manuscript, *Caroline*, at the age of twenty-three and with its publication became an overnight sensation. She has secured an impressive following of loyal fans, many of whom believe she is the successor to Kathleen Woodiwiss.

Cynthia began building the foundation for her future career in the fifth grade, progressing from *Herbert the Talking Diary* to writing a lengthy sequel to *Gone with the Wind* when she was fourteen. It was only two years later in high school that Cynthia met her "Mr. Wright"—Richard Wright. She boasts that she was as much in love as any of her heroines have ever been. They were married on her nineteenth birthday, and consequently Cynthia became a navy wife. Always on the move, their daughter was conceived in Idaho and born in Lawrence, Kansas. While housebound as a young mother, Cynthia wrote and sold *Caroline*.

The key to Cynthia's success might be found in the respect she demonstrates for her readers as well as for the characters she creates. She will not allow anything to happen to her heroines that she could not live with herself. The cornerstone in each of Cynthia's novels is their penetrating focus on one extremely intense relationship. As the curator of such a relationship, Cynthia feels as if she is really involved in one herself. Often she becomes so attached to her fictional couples that, to the delight of her followers, she is inclined to bring them back for cameo appearances in succeeding books. In fact, *Your First Romance* gave Cynthia a perfect opportunity to bring back two characters from *Caroline*. Although Antonia and Jean-Philippe were originally only briefly introduced (as the hero's parents), they captured the readers' interest and desire for more.

When Romance is written well, it's like magic, declares Cynthia. To achieve this, authors must sincerely involve their hearts in their work. According to Cynthia, the secret cannot be taught or explained. If the magic is there, the author can sense it—and so will the readers. Cynthia tells beginning writers not to write a Romance just to make money. She contends there is more at stake than the first sale and eventual royalty statement. There is one's reputation and self-esteem.

With her family's frequent long-distance moves, Cynthia averages one year to write a book of about 400 pages. She now lives in Washington State with her ten-year-old daughter, Jenna, and her loving husband, who is the navigation officer on the Trident submarine *Florida*.

*Pen names:*

Devon Lindsay

*Works include:*

*Caroline* (1977)
*Touch the Sun* (1978)
*Silver Storm* (1979)
*Crimson Intrigue* (1981, as Devon Lindsay)
*Spring Fires* (1983)
*You and No Other* (1984)

# Pirate's Prize

## by Cynthia Wright

and_____
*(your name here)*

"I apologize if I've kept you waiting, mademoiselle. Allow me to introduce myself. Jean-Philippe Beauvisage, at your service." Flashing a grin, the pirate captain stepped into his cabin and closed the door. Though grimy after the long sea battle, he was recklessly handsome: tall and lean-muscled with bronzed skin, keen blue eyes, and wind-ruffled hair as black as midnight. "It's rare for a captured ship to yield a prize as priceless as you. I'm quite pleased. . . ."

"Well, I am not! I demand that you return me to my ship immediately!" Antonia Karsavina looked brave, green eyes sparkling with indignation as she tossed her abundant chestnut curls, but in reality she was terrified. How could this be happening? Just a few hours ago she had been caught up in the innocent pleasure of sailing on Russia's most luxurious passenger vessel, en route for the American colonies and an extended visit with her brother and his family in the town of Boston. When this uncivilized pirate and his crew had attacked her ship, the order went out that no passengers were to be harmed . . . only valuables would be confiscated. Unfortunately, Beauvisage had seen Antonia and decided that she was simply too exquisite to leave behind.

"I'm sorry to disappoint you, mademoiselle," he was saying mockingly as he advanced toward her, "but we lost sight of your ship hours ago. I fear that you shall have to make the best of our situation!"

"But—" Antonia wondered wildly how to save herself from this rogue. Backing up, she felt her knees strike something hard—and then she was sprawling across the captain's bunk.

"Can't wait, eh?" Beauvisage laughed. "You'll have to be patient until I've bathed—but do feel free to undress in the meantime!"

*(continue story . . .)*

*(continue story . . .)*

Coming up behind her husband, Antonia Beauvisage slipped delicate arms around his waist and leaned contentedly against the broad expanse of his back. "Sneaking a look at your new daughter again?"

"I just can't believe it!" Jean-Philippe's whisper was incredulous as he stared down at the tiny sleeping baby. "She's so beautiful—and we actually *created* her!"

"And I was afraid that you'd be bored with life as a shipbuilder in Philadelphia!" Antonia spoke only half in jest. "You don't miss the sea—the excitement—and all that pirate's plunder?"

He turned and lifted his wife up in unyielding arms, capturing her mouth in a heartfelt kiss. "Ah, *chérie*, how could I?" Jean-Philippe murmured at length. "I know that I was stubborn and slow to admit the truth, but finally it did dawn on me that you were plunder enough to occupy me for a lifetime. . . ."

# Romance
# Twenty

# ABOUT THE AUTHOR

## *Jennifer Wilde (Tom E. Huff)*
### (b. 1940)

*It is, of course, necessary for male writers of historical romance to use a feminine pseudonym—just as female writers of Westerns and hardboiled detective fiction must use male names. . . . Would you buy a Western called* Shoot-Out at Blood Gulch *by 'Mary Jane Smith'?*

Jennifer Wilde, by far one of the biggest names in Historical Romance, is a pen name of the most successful male author in the genre—Tom E. Huff. His fans, numbering in the millions all over the world, claim that he conveys a sensuality that few female authors equal. The attraction also lies in the action, vigor, and virility his stories possess. But more than anything, Jennifer Wilde books are solid novels that promise to satisfy.

For seven years Tom had been a writer for a Texas newspaper for which he did weekly reviews, wrote celebrity interviews, and produced a column on paperback books. His exposure to the book world prompted him to try it firsthand. He published over twenty mysteries and contemporary novels under various pseudonyms, and notably is the author of the critically acclaimed *Mirabelle*.

Tom switched to Historical Romance purely by chance. Due to his publisher's concern for "marketing psychology," it was necessary for a decisive name change. He recalls that "Jennifer Wilde" was a product named by a committee in search of something that sounded both sexy and aristocratic. With Jennifer, they struck gold! Since Tom had not read any of the new crop of Historicals, *Love's Tender Fury* had an originality of approach that helped it sell over three million copies in America and another four million in over a dozen foreign countries.

Atmosphere and anticipation are key elements found in Tom's novels. They are intricately woven throughout the plot to create what he calls an aura of sex. Quality always takes precedence over quantity. Tom believes that a few scenes that have been carefully set up are far more effective than a profusion of "sex scenes." He goes to great lengths to prepare a love scene— and then he makes certain it is truly experienced through all the senses.

According to Tom, there is no formula for writing a successful Romance. He suggests that *all* good novels are about real, living people with whom the reader can identify and empathize. Also, they are set against a vivid background that is convincingly presented with accurate detail. He recommends that the story reflect the author's own interests and insights into human nature. His advice to the beginning writer is to read biographies, observe people, learn what motivates them, and what makes them unique. Then utilize that knowledge when creating the characters. A great Romance, Tom asserts, is literate, lively, exciting, emotionally moving, entertaining, and informative.

Tom spends long hours with Jennifer, completely isolated in a third-floor attic study. He writes from 11 A.M. until midnight, taking a break only twice when he swims half a mile. It takes him between twelve and eighteen months to complete a Jennifer Wilde novel. During that time he will devote himself totally to his work, seeing no one, going nowhere. Between books he will socialize and travel, while Jennifer inevitably makes her way onto the best-seller lists.

*Pen names:*

Jennifer Wilde

*Works include:*

*Love's Tender Fury* (1976)
*Dare to Love* (1978)
*Love Me, Marietta* (1981)
*Once More, Miranda* (1983)

*They Call Her Dana*

by Jennifer Wilde

and_____
*(your name here)*

It was a glorious specimen, pale mauve-white lightly veined with gold, the petals incredibly fragile. Jean Pierre Lafarge had never come this deep into the swamps before, and he was elated at his good fortune today. Botany was an eccentric hobby for a virile and handsome young aristocrat—duels, drinking and wenching were the usual pastimes of his set—but, at twenty-four, Jean Pierre found far more excitement in an unknown plant than in any of the lush and lovely belles who hoped to lead him to the altar. Stern, independent, with a reputation for ruthlessness at the gaming tables, he was the despair of his parents, whose plantation, mansion in New Orleans and astonishing wealth made their only son by far the most eligible bachelor in the area. Settling down on the mossy bank with watercolors and sketchpad in hand, he prepared to capture the flower on paper and was soon completely immersed in the task.

He had no idea how much time had passed before he became aware that someone was watching him. It was an acute sensation, almost physical. He put down the pad, set brush aside and slowly, casually, climbed to his feet, his tall, athletic body tightening imperceptibly. The veteran of many a brawl, Jean Pierre had no doubts about his ability to defend himself, but, unlike most of his crowd, he had no taste for fighting and avoided it whenever possible. Staring idly at the bank of ferns, he curled his fists loosely, waiting, and almost a minute passed before the ferns rustled and the girl stepped out.

She couldn't be more than eighteen, he thought, and she was probably younger than that. Tall and slender, with a deliciously voluptuous body accentuated by the soiled and tattered pink cotton dress, she had thick, filthy honey-blonde hair, frightened brown eyes and a full, provocative mouth. There was a bruise on her left cheekbone, scratches on her bare shoulders. She stood there in front of the ferns like a young doe, silent, poised for flight, and he saw that she was trembling.

"Don't be afraid," he said. "I'm not going to hurt you. Who are you, child?"

"My—my name is Dana," she replied. "They—you gotta help me, sir. They wanna—my step pa and his two sons. They wanna—my ma passed on, you see, and now they think they kin—"

She paused, tears welling over long, curling lashes, and Jean Pierre didn't need to hear any more. He knew full well what the brutes wanted to do, and looking at this amazingly beautiful child of the swamps, he knew why.

"You gotta help me," she pleaded. "I caint go—go back there. Could you take me to New Awe-leans—?"

---

*(continue story . . .)*

_____

_____

_____

_____

_____

_____

_____

*(continue story . . .)*

*(continue story . . .)*

The storm was raging outside, the worst Natchez had seen in years, but that didn't matter. She would ride through a hurricane if necessary. He was waiting for her, and she knew—at last she knew—she couldn't bear to live without him. Moving quickly down the elegant staircase, the skirts of her exquisite gown making a silken rustle, Dana threw open the door. The crystal chandelier in the hall tinkled loudly as a gust of wind swept past her. Yes, she would go to him. She might rue the day, probably would, but all the wealth, all the luxury in the world meant nothing without Stephen Blackmon. Unhooking the glittering diamond necklace, removing it from her throat, she gazed at the fiery gems for a long moment, then tossed the necklace into the hall and hurried out into the storm.

# Romance Twenty-One

# ABOUT THE AUTHOR

_____

## (b.     )

One of today's most promising up-and-coming writers of Romance,

_____, is sure to take _____ place among
*(your name)*                                 *(his/her)*

the great Romance writers of our time. Already, _____ has
*(your first name)*

collaborated on a number of popular works with such renowned authors as

Jennifer Blake, Johanna Lindsey, and Patricia Matthews. _____ first
*(His/Her)*

Romance, _Legacy   of   Desire,_   which   was   about

_____, was considered a _____
*(story summary)*                                        *(adjective)*

work. The ____ _____ acclaimed _____ as one of the
*(favorite newspaper)*                       *(your first name)*

most _____ writers in the Romance genre, second only to
*(adjective)*

_____. _____ __ prefers to write in
*(your favorite Romance writer)*                *(your first name)*

the _____ and averages _____ pages a day. _____ secret to
*(time of day)*                   *(number)*                            *(His/Her)*

writing     a     successful     Romance     is     simply     to

_____. Currently, _____ lives with
           *(your secret)*                                      *(he/she)*

_____ _____
                    *(name of relative, friend or lover)*

in _____.
       *(city/state)*

## Pen names:
*(fill in below)*

## Works include:

*Legacy of Desire*
*Love's Seeking Heart*
*Alicia*
*Passion's Fire*
*Lane End House*
*Love's Persuading*
*Conspired Seduction*
*Wings of Love*
*My Lady Cinderella*
*Shadow of the Past*
*Boundary Lines*
*Kate of Clyve Shore*
*Love's Savage Desire*
*Bold Passion's Price*
*Yankee Duchess*
*Love Wears Only One Face*
*The Panther Feast*
*Disobedient Daughter*
*Pirate's Prize*
*They Call Her Dana*

_____

_(YOUR NAME)_

_____

_(title of your Romance)_

by _____

_(your name)_

and _____

_(name of coauthor)_

_(write opening paragraphs . . .)_

_____

_____

_____

_____

_____

_____

_____

_____

_____

_____

_____

_____

_____

_____

*(continue opening paragraphs . . .)*

*(continue story . . .)*

_____

_____

_____

_____

_____

_____

_____

_____

_____

_____

_____

_____

_____

_____

_____

_____

_____

_____

*(continue story . . .)*

_____

_____

_____

_____

_____

_____

_____

_____

_____

_____

_____

_____

_____

_____

_____

_____

_____

_____

_____

_____

_____

_____

*(YOUR NAME)*

*(write closing paragraphs . . .)*

_____

_____

_____

_____

_____

_____

_____

_____

_____

_____

_____

_____

_____

_____

_____

_____

_____

_____

_____

*(continue closing paragraphs . . .)*

# *Your First Sale*

By now you may be seriously thinking about selling a Romance of your own. Review the Directory of Major Romance Publishers at the back of this book. Study the market, choose the publisher best suited to your style, and write for that publisher's most recent requirements. These guidelines will point you in the right direction and keep you in line. Be sure to read Kathryn Falk's *How to Write a Romance and Get It Published* and the other books listed under Recommended Reading.

You will find that many Romance publishers provide up-to-date "tip sheets" for would-be writers. These tip sheets detail the publishers' specific ingredients for each line of Romance books. We have included here three sample tip sheets. Harlequin and Candlelight/Ecstasy are offered as tip sheet examples from two popular Category Romance publishers. Scarlet Ribbons' guidelines will give you an idea of what is required by an Historical Romance line. Read them over. Familiarize yourself with their formats and the type of information they contain.

Of course, all Romance lines are different, so it will be necessary to write to each of your chosen publishers individually. Though many publishers have formal tip sheets, others do not. In those instances, a letter of query should be written. Remember, always include an SASE (self-addressed stamped envelope).

Onward and upward . . .

# *Sample Tip Sheets*

Dell Publishing Co., Inc. • 1 Dag Hammarskjold Plaza • 245 East 47 Street • New York, NY 10017 •

TO WHOM IT MAY CONCERN:

Thank you for your interest in the Dell Candlelight Ecstasy Romance line. Though there are no hard and fast rules for our line in regard to plot, characterization etc., there are a few things to keep in mind if you're submitting a manuscript for our consideration.

Most Ecstasy heroines are between the ages of 25 and 35, most are established in an interesting career.  Avoid the use of formula plot devices such as a marriage of convenience between the protagonists, or amnesia.  These romances are essentially sensuous, realistic contemporary stories set in the United States. We prefer that writers focus on developing the relationship between the hero and heroine and that conflicts in the story arise out of this relationship (ie:  career vs. marriage, unresolved feelings regarding a prior relationship, etc.). Love scenes should be tastefully handled without being pornographic, or overly explicit.

We will consider completed manuscripts of 50,000 to 60,000 words (approximately 200 to 225 typewritten, double-spaced pages)  or partials of 50 to 70 pages in length, containing a detailed synopsis and outline.

Good luck in your writing.  We hope to hear from you soon!

**Dell**

Dell Publishing Co. Inc. · 1 Dag Hammarskjold Plaza · 245 East 47 Street · New York, NY 10017 ·

First and foremost, Ecstasy Romances must depict a compelling love story. The relationship must be realistically developed and bring into play all the channels of communication that are operating between two people in love. Yes, we want smoldering love scenes. But we also want to see our hero and heroine finding their way to each other through emotional and intellectual encounters as well. In other words, we want to see the emergence of a convincing, full-dimensioned and mature love affair.

Though the books certainly incorporate elements of romantic fantasy, it is fantasy grounded in reality. Ecstasy romances differ from the standard "sweet" romances, not only in terms of sensuous detail or extended love scenes, but in terms of characterization, motivation and plot. We are looking for warm appealing characters that have been rendered with insight and texture; characters that a reader will care about.

Though we have no rigid guidelines regarding the placement and content of love scenes, we do feel that    sexual chemistry and emotional involvement do bring men and women together in the most wonderful ways. Sensuous, non-explicit presentation of this side of a love affair should be part of an Ecstasy Romance. But whether the encounter is a quick kiss on her fingertips, or a night of passion, the scene is always one of idealized love; the emphasis is on a seduction of the senses (taste, smell, touch) and an intense, convincing emotional exchange between the protagonists.

In any case, let me advise those who wish to submit a manuscript to us to first read a wide selection of our books. Good luck!

Anne Gisonny
Senior Editor
Candlelight Romances

**Dell**

145

WORLDWIDE LIBRARY SUPERROMANCE

EDITORIAL GUIDELINES

<u>Length</u>:   95,000 words.

The overall objective of Superromance is to produce good solid reads with a contemporary
tone (i.e. language, situations, characters and so forth), using romance as the major
theme.  To achieve this, emphasis should be placed on individual writing styles and
unique ideas.  (No previously published work will be reprinted as a Superromance.)

<u>Heroine</u>:

Generally in her mid to late twenties, she should have a fairly clear idea of who she
is as an <u>individual</u> and of her own self worth.  Thus, due to her intelligence, maturity
and gutsiness, she can certainly stand up for herself.  If she has an important character
flaw, it should be something she is aware of from the beginning of the story and learns
to deal with in a constructive fashion.  The Superromance heroine is most often from
North America.  If not, then the hero should be.  She may be single, widowed or divorced.
She should have a credible career about which the author can write with insight and
authority.  Lastly, the Superromance heroine is now ready to share her life and
her love with the hero.

<u>Hero</u>:

Handsome, passionate, self-assured, older than the heroine, he is a man who will
ultimately be successful if he is not so already.  While he doesn't have to be super
macho, he must be a strong, sexy man, capable of tenderness, with his own needs and
vulnerabilities.  He can be single, widowed or divorced.  He may be a North American
or a foreigner.  Never should he be physically abusive.

<u>Plot</u>:

The story should revolve around multidimensional characters.  It is told predominantly
from the heroine's point of view, but the hero's perspective is welcome, too.  The
plot should be complex and imaginative enough to sustain reader interest over 95,000
words, without forsaking realism.  Ultimately, a Superromance must be uplifting.

Subplots and secondary characters (preferably not children) <u>must</u> affect the major
story line, but they should be interesting, emotionally moving or suspenseful in
their own right.

The growing relationship between the hero and heroine should be based on more than
pure physical attraction.  Conflicts should have emotional depth, rather than result
from convenient misunderstandings or superficial personality clashes.  The realistic
problems--and solutions--facing men and women today should be explored.  Again, we
are looking for a freshness of approach.

# SAMPLE TIP SHEETS

Locale:

Either North American or foreign, the only criterion being that the setting is romantic and described in a natural way, rather than reading like a travelogue.

Style:

Correct grammar and American spelling, except where improper usage is important to the depiction of the character. Please refer to the Chicago Manual of Style or Webster's New Collegiate Dictionary for detail questions.

Dialogue that is to the point, moves the plot forward, shades a character or develops the relationship is essential. Non-relevant information in either dialogue or narrative will be cut.

Sex:

It may be explicit as long as it's written in good taste. Sex may be frequent, although it should never be gratuitous. The emphasis should be on shared sensual feelings. And don't forget the romantic aspects of relationships. Modern attitudes toward sex should be reflected while reinforcing the values of love, caring or commitment.

Summary:

The criteria for Superromance is flexible aside from length. The determining factor for publication will always be quality. Authors should strive to break free of stereotypes, cliches and worn plot devices to create strong believable stories with depth and emotional intensity. Superromances are intended to appeal to a wide range of romance readers.

A general familiarity with current romance fiction is advisable, to keep abreast of ever-changing trends and of overall scope. But we don't want imitations and we are open for newness--sincere, heartfelt writing based on true-to-life experiences and fantasies the reader can identify with.

The line is based on a mixture of new, as well as established authors. Contract terms are the same for both agented and nonagented authors.

Submission Format:

For a new author--as complete a manuscript as possible, accompanied by a detailed synopsis of the balance.

For previously published authors--three chapters plus a long synopsis (approximately 20 pages), plus a copy of the author's most recently published book.

For authors the Superromance staff has worked with before--three chapters plus a lengthy synopsis.

Finally, please clearly mark "Superromance" on your submission and direct it to the attention of:

> Star Helmer
> Editorial Director
> Superromance
> Worldwide Library
> 225 Duncan Mill Road
> Don Mills, Ontario
> Canada    M3B 3K9

SCARLET RIBBONS GUIDELINES
Signet Historical Romance Line

LENGTH:        125,000-150,000 words

SETTING:       No specific guidelines

TIME PERIOD:   1066 - World War I

POINT OF VIEW:  The story is told in the third person, largely from
       the heroine's point of view, although some scenes may be written
       from the hero's point of view.

HERO AND HEROINE:  The heroine should be young and, if not American,
       partly or wholly of a nationality with which the reader can
       identify--such as Scottish, English, or Irish.  She should also
       be intelligent, strong willed, and independent, a character not
       easily discouraged.

       The hero should be slightly older and also of a similar nationality.

PLOT:  The story must focus on a strong central romance.  We do not
       want the hero and heroine to be separated for the bulk of the book;
       the heroine should not sleep with numerous other men; and violence
       should be kept to a minimum.  Rape, except in vertain very special
       circumstances of the heroine by the hero, is to be avoided.  Definitely
       NO gang rapes!

HOW TO SUBMIT: Submissions are welcome from unagented and novice writers
       as well as from published authors.  We prefer complete manuscripts,
       but will accept three sample chapters and an outline, including
       a full plot synopsis and thorough descriptions of the main characters
       and setting.  Published writers should send a resume of their works.
       Payment depends on the author's track record and past experience.

MANUSCRIPT PREPARATION:  Please leave one-inch margins on both sides
       of the page.  The manuscript should be neat, well-typed, double-
       spaced on standard-sized plain white bond paper.  DO NOT use
       onion-skin, color, eraseable, or odd-sized paper.  Polish your
       work, proofread it carefully, and send us your best.

       Please enclose a stamped, self-addressed manilla envelope with
       your submission.  Be sure to keep a file copy of everything you
       submit, including the manuscript.  Study our guidelines and other
       Signet historical romances.  And please make sure the work you
       submit meets with the requirements outlined above.

# Directory of Major Romance Publishers

Ballantine Books, Inc.
201 East 50 Street
New York, NY 10022
Attn: Pamela Dean Strickler
(Contemporary/Historical)

Bantam Books Inc.
666 Fifth Avenue
New York, NY 10103
Attn: Carolyn Nichols
(Contemporary/Romantic Suspense)
Attn: Linda Price
(Historical)

The Berkley Publishing Corp.
200 Madison Avenue
New York, NY 10016
Attn: Nancy Coffey
(Contemporary/Historical/Regency)

Candlelight Ecstasy Romance and Ecstasy
    Supreme
Dell Publishing Co. Inc.
1 Dag Hammarskjold Plaza
245 East 47 Street
New York, NY 10017
Attn: Anne Gisonny
(Category)*

Caprice Romances (Tempo Books)
Berkley Publishing Corp.
200 Madison Avenue
New York, NY 10016
Attn: Betty Ann Crawford
(Teen)*

Dell Publishing Co. Inc.
1 Dag Hammerskjold Plaza
245 East 47 Street
New York, NY 10017
Attn: Susan Spano
(Contemporary/Historical)

Fawcett Books
201 East 50 Street
New York, NY 10022
Attn: Michaela Hamilton
(Contemporary/Historical)
Attn: Leona Nevler
(Regency)

First Love from Silhouette
Silhouette Books
1230 Avenue of the Americas
New York, NY 10020
Attn: Nancy Jackson
(Teen)

---

*Indicates that publisher provides tip sheet. A query letter should be submitted to all other publishers.

Flare Novels
Avon Books
959 Eighth Avenue
New York, NY 10019
Attn: Judy Gitenstein
(Teen)

Harlequin American Romance
Harlequin Books
919 Third Avenue (15th floor)
New York, NY 10022
Attn: Hilari Cohen or Debra Matteucci
(Category)*

Harlequin Presents
Mills & Boon Ltd.
15–16 Brook's Mews
London, England
W1A 1DR
Attn: Jacqui Bianchi
(Category)*

Harlequin Romance
Mills & Boon Ltd.
15–16 Brook's Mews
London, England
W1A 1DR
Attn: Jacqui Bianchi
(Category)*

Harlequin Temptation
Harlequin Books
225 Duncan Mill Road
Don Mills, Ontario
Canada M3B 3K9
Attn: Kay Meierbachtol
(Category)

Hodder and Stoughton
P.O. Box 703
Mill Road
Dunton Green
Sevenoaks
Kent TN13 2YA
England
Attn: Mary Loring
(Contemporary)

Hourglass Romances
Zebra Books Inc.
475 Park Avenue South
New York, NY 10016
Attn: Kathy O'Herir
(Category)*

Laurel Leaf Young Love
Dell Publishing Co. Inc.
1 Dag Hammarskjold Plaza
New York, NY 10017
Attn: The Editors
(Teen)

Loveswept
Bantam Books Inc.
666 Fifth Avenue
New York, NY 10103
Attn: Carolyn Nichols
(Category)*

Masquerade
Mills & Boon
15–16 Brook's Mews
London, England
W1A 1DR
Attn: Heather Jeeves
(Historical)

---

*Indicates that publisher provides tip sheet. A query letter should be submitted to all other publishers.

Pinnacle Books Inc.
1430 Broadway
New York, NY 10018
Attn: Sondra Ordover
(Historical)

Pocket Books
1230 Avenue of the Americas
New York, NY 10020
Attn: Kate Duffy
(Historical)

Rapture Romance
The New American Library Inc./Signet
1633 Broadway
New York, NY 10019
Attn: Robin Grunder
(Category)*

Robert Hale
Clerkenwell House
45–47 Clerkenwell Green
London, England
EC1R OHT
Attn: John Hale
(Contemporary*/Historical/Regency)

Scarlet Ribbons
The New American Library Inc./Signet
1633 Broadway
New York, NY 10019
Attn: Hilary Ross
(Historical)*

Second Chance at Love
Berkley Publishing Corp.
200 Madison Avenue
New York, NY 10016
Attn: Ellen Edwards
(Category)*

Serenade Books
The Zondervan Corp.
749 Templeton Drive
Nashville, TN 37205
Attn: Anne Severance
(Contemporary Inspirational)*

Serenade Saga Books
The Zondervan Corp.
749 Templeton Drive
Nashville, TN 37205
Attn: Anne Severance
(Historical Inspirational)*

Signet Regency Romance
The New American Library Inc./Signet
1633 Broadway
New York, NY 10019
Attn: Hilary Ross
(Regency)*

Silhouette Desire
Silhouette Books
1230 Avenue of the Americas
New York, NY 10020
Attn: Karen Solem
(Category)

Silhouette Inspiration
Silhouette Books
1230 Avenue of the Americas
New York, NY 10020
Attn: Karen Solem
(Contemporary Inspirational)

Silhouette Intimate Moments
Silhouette Books
1230 Avenue of the Americas
New York, NY 10020
Attn: Karen Solem
(Category)

---

*Indicates that publisher provides tip sheet. A query letter should be submitted to all other publishers.

Silhouette Romances
Silhouette Books
1230 Avenue of the Americas
New York, NY 10020
Attn: Karen Solem
(Category)

Silhouette Special Editions
Silhouette Books
1230 Avenue of the Americas
New York, NY 10020
Attn: Karen Solem
(Category)

Starlight Romances
Doubleday and Co. Inc.
245 Park Avenue
New York, NY 10167
Attn: Veronica Mixon
(Regency)*

Superromance
Harlequin Books
225 Duncan Mill Road
Don Mills, Ontario
Canada M3B 3K9
Attn: Star Helmer
(Category)*

Sweet Dreams
Bantam Books
Cloverdale Press Inc.
133 Fifth Avenue
New York, NY 10003
Attn: Ben Baglio
(Teen)*

Tapestry Romance
Pocket Books
1230 Avenue of the Americas
New York, NY 10020
Attn: Kate Duffy
(Historical)

To Have and to Hold
Berkley Publishing Corp.
200 Madison Avenue (15th floor)
New York, NY 10016
Attn: Ellen Edwards
(Category)*

Vista Romance
The New American Library Inc./Signet
1633 Broadway
New York, NY 10019
Attn: Cindy Kane
(Teen)*

Walker & Co.
720 Fifth Avenue
New York, NY 10019
Attn: Ruth Cavin
(Regency)

Warner Books Inc.
666 Fifth Avenue
New York, NY 10103
Attn: Fredda Isaacson
(Historical)

Wildfire and Windswept
Scholastic Inc.
730 Broadway
New York, NY 10003
Attn: Ann Reit
(Teen)

*Indicates that publisher provides tip sheet. A query letter should be submitted to all other publishers.

Worldwide Library "Best Sellers"
Worldwide Library
225 Duncan Mill Road
Don Mills, Ontario
Canada M3B 3K9
Attn: Jennifer Campbell
(Contemporary/Historical)*

Zebra Books
475 Park Avenue South
New York, NY 10016
Attn: Leslie Gelbman
(Historical)*

*Indicates that publisher provides tip sheet. A query letter should be submitted to all other publishers.

# Recommended Reading

Barnhart, Helene Schellenberg. *Writing Romance Fiction for Love and Money*. Cincinnati: Writer's Digest Books, 1983.

Falk, Kathryn. *How to Write a Romance and Get It Published*. New York: Crown, 1983.

———. *Love's Leading Ladies*. New York: Crown, 1982.

Lowery, Marilyn M. *How to Write Romance Novels That Sell*. New York: Rawson Associates, 1983.

MacManus, Yvonne. *You Can Write a Romance! And Get It Published!* New York: Pocket Books, 1983.